An Uncommon Story

Ivan Goncharov

Translated by Stephen Pearl

Edited and annotated
by Alessandro Gallenzi

ALMA CLASSICS

ALMA CLASSICS
an imprint of

ALMA BOOKS LTD
Thornton House
Thornton Road
Wimbledon Village
London SW19 4NG
United Kingdom
www.almaclassics.com

An Uncommon Story first published in Russian 1924
This edition first published by Alma Classics in 2023

Cover: David Wardle

Translation © Stephen Pearl, 2023
Notes © Alma Books Ltd

Printed in Great Britain by CPI Group (UK) Ltd, Croydon CR0 4YY

ISBN: 978-1-84749-902-8

Contents

An Uncommon Story

An Uncommon Story	1
An Uncommon Story – Continued	143
Note to *An Uncommon Story*	153
Supplement to *An Uncommon Story*	159
Notes	161

An Uncommon Story

In 1846 when I first met Belinsky and his circle of writers and friends,* three of them were not present: Turgenev, Botkin and Annenkov.* The last two were abroad, and Turgenev apparently in a village somewhere. They often came up in conversation within Belinsky's circle, which included Panayev, Grigorovich,* Nekrasov, Dostoevsky (who came with his short novel, *Poor People*). Later the group was joined by Druzhinin with his short novel *Polinka Saks*.* Others who attended included some who were not writers themselves: Tyutchev, Maslov, Yazykov.* I had met Panayev and Yazykov before at Maykov's, the poet's father.* It was through Yazykov that I had sent Belinsky my novel *The Same Old Story** for him to read and for his opinion as to whether it was acceptable and whether I should continue with the second part. The novel was conceived in 1844 and written in 1845, except for a few chapters which were left for me to complete in 1846. It took Belinsky three months to read, and whenever I met him he would praise my work effusively and predicted great success in the future. He mentioned it to everyone he met, so that long before the novel appeared in print everyone had heard about it, including the public at large – not only in the literary circles of Moscow and St Petersburg. We would all meet most often at Panayev's and Yazykov's place, as well at times at Tyutchev's place, which was spacious enough to accommodate the whole crowd. We would meet at Belinsky's almost every day, but not all of us – he didn't have enough room. In the summer of 1846 everyone left town – Belinsky, I believe, for the Crimea, Panayev and Nekrasov for Kazan – and in the autumn we all reassembled in St Petersburg. At that time, our circle left Krayevsky and *Otechestvenniye Zapiski*,* and all of us followed

Belinsky over to the *Sovremennik*,* which had been taken over by
Panayev and Nekrasov, who moved into the same house. Once,
in 1847, it was said that Turgenev had come there. I happened
to drop in one evening at Belinsky's and found Turgenev there.
Even at that time, I recall, he had already published something in
Otechestvenniye Zapiski.* Members of our circle were speaking
of him as a gifted and promising writer. He was standing with
his back to the door through which I entered, and was inspecting some engravings or portraits on the wall through a lorgnette.
Belinsky introduced us to each other; Turgenev turned round and
offered me his hand and then turned back to resume his scrutiny
of the portraits. He then turned back to face me and made a few
complimentary remarks about my novel before turning back to the
portraits. It's clear to me that he was putting on an act, preening
himself, posing as a dandy, an Onegin or a Pechorin,* aping their
manner and bearing. Later, at moments of candour, he would
confess to being consumed with envy of those who were lionized
in the upper reaches of society – Stolypin (nicknamed "Mongo")*
and the poet Lermontov – when he happened to encounter them.
I was watching him while he continued to go through the motions
of inspecting the paintings, which were, of course, familiar to
all Belinsky's friends, who were all regular visitors. I paid close
attention to his facial features, which I found unattractive, in
particular his nose, big mouth and puffy lips, and most of all his
chin – all of which made him appear niggardly and tight-fisted.
What particularly struck me was the way his voice kept on changing – sometimes irritatingly squeaky and effeminate and at other
times weak with a hint of a lisp, like that of a much older man.
His eyes, however, were most expressive, and his head large, while
his body was well-proportioned, and altogether he presented a
healthy and robust appearance. His hair was shoulder-length.
Later, after he had turned grey, he began to sport a beard, which
masked his weak chin and unattractive mouth. I don't have a
very clear memory of the years 1846 and 1847: was Turgenev still
there at the time, or even in 1848, after Botkin and Annenkov had

arrived, or had he already left? All I remember for sure is that it was in 1848 that Belinsky died, and in addition to that loss, the whole circle began to be subjected to increasingly severe censorship because of revolution and a change of government in France.* It was at that time that the Moscow writers Granovsky, Kavelin and Galakhov,* I believe, visited St Petersburg. At that time too, Herzen happened to be passing through, and I ran into him at the Wulf pastry shop, and we were introduced by Panayev, who was with him, but we only managed to exchange a few words. He was going abroad, and I never saw him again after that. But I'll leave it at that. I have simply given just enough of a description of the circumstances for the purposes of this narrative, whose protagonist is Turgenev, my association with him and its consequences. Perhaps this rough-and-ready but truthful account will make clear what it was that has driven me, almost against my will, to write these pages. Turgenev would come and go to St Petersburg, sometimes staying for a whole winter. While his mother was alive, as he explained, and limited his financial resources, his lifestyle was relatively frugal, but after her death it became more expansive. He employed a cook and started to invite guests for dinner, and his reputation grew both as a host and a writer. Everyone continued to foregather at his place, and at Druzhinin's, Tyutchev's and Yazykov's, including Annenkov and Botkin. Turgenev was everyone's favourite, not just for his intelligence, talent and education, but also for his good-natured, ingratiating friendliness. The moment he met anyone, he would treat that person as his very best friend, put his arm around his shoulder, call him "my dear...", regard him with warmth in his eyes and bathe him in even warmer conversation, indulge him in any request, go to see him and invite him home. But the moment he took leave of him, he would forget him and open his arms to the next one. When he was invited somewhere, he was sure to turn up, and sometimes, after receiving a visitor, he would accompany him to where he was next going to call. He acted in this way because of the easygoing and laid-back, even carefree, absent-minded character he liked to pose as. People would say of him good-humouredly: "He invited me and then went out somewhere! Well, after all he's an artist – talented!" And he would be forgiven! What astonishment then shone in his eyes, as if he had somehow quite forgotten what he may have said or promised! His promises to show up somewhere were not often kept: he would make a promise and then, if he happened to get a better offer, that's where he would go. And later, if he ran into the person whom he had let down, he would clap his hand to his head and put on such a convincing and shamefaced show of forgetfulness. But when there was somewhere he really wanted to go, he never forgot.

It was in 1848, or even earlier, in 1847, when I first conceived the notion of *Oblomov*.* I would quite unsystematically jot down some notes on paper, sometimes just a single word to remind me of a whole sentence, or a brief phrase or two suggesting a whole scene. A felicitous turn of phrase would occur to me, or I would scrawl the kernel of an outline on half a page, and sometimes a sketch of a character. In this way I would accumulate a heap of pages or scraps of paper, and a novel would unfurl itself in my head. On rare occasions I would sit down and in a week or two produce two or three chapters and then leave them aside. I completed the first part in 1850. But in 1848 in the "Illustrated Almanac" in the *Sovremennik*, I had already published 'Oblomov's Dream'.* At that time I had the bad habit of recounting to all and sundry whatever I had in mind, what I was writing and reading. To anyone who called on me I would show whatever I had already written, and even told them what I intended to add. The reason for this was that I was simply bursting with a wealth of ideas and couldn't contain myself – not to mention the fact that I was totally lacking in self-confidence. I never stopped questioning and tormenting myself: "Am I just writing garbage? Is it any good? Is it nonsense?" It was with immense trepidation that I handed over *The Same Old Story* to Belinsky for one of his gatherings, without even knowing what I thought of it myself – and I still don't even now. As soon as I sit down to write I am already tormented by doubts. Even when I was approached to translate what was already in print into a foreign language, I refused. "It's not good enough," I thought. "Why should I stick my neck out?" So I went about canvassing the opinions of all and sundry about my work, and was careful to take note of them, but realized I was making a pest of myself in the process. I got sick of all the time I spent making plans and trying to disentangle the relationships among all the relevant people, and assess what progress I was making. I wrote slowly because my imagination couldn't conjure up one single character or one single action, but rather a whole landscape, complete with towns, villages, woods and a crowd of characters, all in one go – in a word, a vast arena buzzing with life. The descent from that mountain was arduous and slow, and it was difficult to pick out details and link them up! My novels, as I have mentioned in another document addressed to "My Critics", embrace major periods of Russian life, for example in *Oblomov* and *Malinovka Heights*,* which cover a period of some thirty years. Among the reasons why it takes me so long to write is a lack of free time, my office work and also my lazy and disorganized lifestyle. Everything I have just written is relevant to my purpose. It was Turgenev, of course, with whom I most often shared the details of my intentions, particularly with regard to *Oblomov*, believing him to be a man of great critical judgement and more willing than most to listen to what I told him about my work. At the time he was writing his well-known *Memoirs of a Hunter*,* filling the *Sovremennik* with one story after another, so that even Belinsky would say (not to his face, but to others including myself): "You would think he's sent in plenty already, but he still keeps them coming!" But those "memoirs" were eagerly read and rightfully contributed to his growing reputation. There was no one who so artistically but in a low-key manner depicted the regime of serfdom and its iniquities, and there was hardly anyone else who painted life in the Russian countryside and nature with such a soft brush and velvet touch! Turgenev's literary reputation as an extraordinary miniaturist will endure. 'Bezhin Meadow', 'The Singers', 'Khor and Kalinych', 'Kasyan' and many, many other miniatures were not so much sketched as sculpted in inimitably exquisite bas-relief. "As a miniaturist," people will say. "But what about his larger works? *A Nest of the Gentry*, *Fathers and Children*, *On the Eve*, *Smoke*.* Can they really be described as miniatures? Aren't they precisely the works which have built and cemented his lofty place in world literature? They are, after all, major, complete and authentic portraits of Russian life!" In response to all this, I will heave a deep sigh and return to my subject.

In 1849, I returned to my birthplace, Simbirsk on the Volga. It was there, during the four summer months, that I gave birth to and developed the large-scale plan for my new novel, *Malinovka Heights*. It had long been known as *The Artist* (that is to say, Raisky). I continued with the work of mentally planning both *Oblomov* and *Malinovka Heights*, filling, as I usually did, piles of scrap paper with notes, pen portraits, events, scenes and so on. In St Petersburg my job kept me busy, and that, together with my laziness, meant that up to 1852 I returned to my writing, that is to say both novels, only rarely. In October that year I embarked on a round-the-world tour aboard the frigate *Pallada*. At sea, apart from my duties as secretary to Admiral Putyatin,* I was also tutoring four marines in literature and history, and was working only on my travel notes, later to be published under the title *The Frigate Pallada*.* I had with me my plans for both novels. I made some additions here and there, but had no time for writing. I was totally taken up with this new world, new lifestyle and new impressions.

At the beginning of 1855, in February to be precise, I returned home via Siberia and St Petersburg. There I found the whole literary circle in session: Turgenev, Annenkov, Botkin, Nekrasov, Panayev, Grigorovich. They were then joined by Count Lev Nikolayevich Tolstoy, who had immediately made a name for himself by his "war stories".* If I am not mistaken, there was also another Count in St Petersburg at the time, Alexei Konstantinovich Tolstoy (who later wrote *The Death of Ivan the Terrible*).* I had made the acquaintance of both of them, although I've forgotten at whose house. I think it was either at Prince Odoevsky's* or Turgenev's. Then Count A. Tolstoy left, while Lev Nikolayevich (I'm not sure whether Count Leo Tolstoy was then in St Petersburg, or it was later) was staying there and met us almost every day at the houses of the same people – Turgenev, Panayev and others. There was a lot of conversation, discussions about literature, convivial dinners – in other words, everyone had a good time. At that time, too, the censorship wasn't so severe.

In 1856 I was offered the post of censor, and I had to accept it. At the time I was publishing my travel writings, and that was diverting my attention from my literary works, *Oblomov* and *Raisky*. It was as early as 1855 that I began to notice that Turgenev was paying me increased attention. He often sought my company, and apparently valued my opinions and listened attentively to what I was saying. This, of course, I found not unpleasant, and I spoke freely, especially about my literary projects. He was particularly attentive when I happened to read something. I was at that time busy sending to the journals chapters from my "traveller's notes", and it was my habit to read to various people my latest writings. I didn't want to burden Turgenev with reading to him these casual descriptions. Nevertheless, I recall that when he learnt that I was going to read some chapter or other at Maykov's, he showed up. In short, he was always around, and we were thus drawn closer to each other, so that I grew accustomed to sharing with him everything I had in mind. Once, for instance, in 1855 as a matter of fact, he came to my flat in Kozhevnikov's* house on the Nevsky Prospekt, near Vladimirsky Prospekt, and continued to pay close attention to the thoughts I was sharing so effusively, and plied me artfully with questions about my plans and intentions. (I had completed Part One and several other chapters of *Oblomov*, which he already knew in detail.) Suddenly, out of the blue, I started revealing to him not only the whole plan of *Malinovka Heights*, my next novel, but even read to him in great detail every scene and every event which I had written down on scraps of paper. "Now listen to what else I have in mind!" I would say. He listened without moving, and almost holding his breath, bending his ear as close as possible to my mouth, and squeezing close to me on the small divan in the corner of my room. When I came to the heart-to-heart talk between Vera and her grandmother, he remarked: "That could be from one of Goethe's novels!" Volokhov, the nihilist, as he appears in the final edition, was then portrayed in my novel as a freethinker who had been exiled and was under police supervision, due to his unreliability. But the "difficult customer", as Volokhov was later depicted in the press, simply didn't exist, because nihilism had not yet made its appearance in the '40s. Persons suspected of being "freethinkers" were sent to the governorates in the provinces. But since the pace of my writing was so slow, my novel had to keep up with the times and change accordingly. Twice in 1862 I was down on the Volga – at that time, Volokhovs similar to the one in my novel were springing up all over the place. In my original plan, Vera, having fallen for Volokhov, had left with him for Siberia, and Raisky had left the country and was travelling abroad, and, returning after several years, found a new generation and a picture of a happy life. Marfenka's children and so on. I had planned a very long chapter about Raisky's forebears, with descriptions of dark and tragic episodes in their family chronicles, beginning with his great grandfather, his grandfather and finally his father. Here there appeared, one after the other, figures of the time of Elizabeth,* a dreaded despot, and on the estate, and in the family, a petty tyrant, a family life rife with violence, mysterious, bloody goings-on, rampant cruelty and outlandish oriental luxury. Next to appear was the figure of a courtier of Catherine the Great* – slim, elegant and debauched by his sybaritic French upbringing, but an educated follower of the Encyclopedists* who had lived out his days on an estate where he divided his time between his French library, a fine cuisine and a harem of peasant women. The last to follow him was a product of the early nineteenth century – a mystic and Mason. Next came a hero and patriot of the years 1812, 1813 and 1814, followed by a "Decembrist*" and others right up until the Raisky of *Malinovka Heights*". I have been telling this story in the same way that people recount their dreams, in such a hurry that they get out of breath. So I'm busily describing the Volga, the bluffs, Vera's trysts on moonlit nights at the foot of the hill and in the garden, her scenes with Volokhov, Raisky and others. I'm enjoying myself and swelling with pride at my fluency, and anxious to meet the challenge of living up to the challenge posed by that keenly critical mind. Turgenev listened as if moribund, without moving. But I could tell that what I was reading was making a great impression on him. I was telling him about Sofya Belovodova and the death of Natasha as if it were a kind of sketch of all these women, each with their own character. I also described at length Kozlov, the teacher, his schooldays and how the other boys made fun of him, even when he was eating and they took his hat and hid it without his noticing. I also described his marriage and how his wife deceived him. In a word, everything, *j'ai vidé mon sac!** Before concluding, I added: "So, if I were dead, you could find a lot here that you could use. But as long as I'm alive I'll do it myself!" Turgenev was careful to question me, and asked whether I had told this to anyone else. I said I hadn't, but soon afterwards, in Turgenev's presence, I told Dudyshkin* the same thing, and also Druzhinin, and repeated it at various receptions. And that, I believe, was it. I still have the letter which Turgenev wrote that he would never forget the scenes, events and so on which I had described to him and Druzhinin. And indeed, as it turned out, he never did! As soon as he got home, he must have written down everything he had heard word for word. Later, of course, I forgot all of this talk, and concentrated on *Oblomov*. In 1857, I went abroad to Marienbad* to take the waters, and in the course of seven weeks completed the last three parts of *Oblomov*, except for three or four chapters. (I had completed the first part earlier.) In my head I had worked out the final version of the novel and put it down on paper virtually from memory. I was writing more than a printer's sheet* a day, which was against doctor's orders. But that didn't deter me. I was overjoyed at the prospect of taking my manuscript to Paris, where I knew I would find Turgenev and Botkin, and where I also found Fet,* who had married Botkin's sister, who lived there. There I read to them various chapters of the last three parts – I was pleased to see that Turgenev had stopped reacting sourly to my readings. "Yes, it may be only a rough draft, but, of course, the structure itself is sound!" He sounded almost dejected, which rather surprised me. But I put that down to the weakness of my pen.

The whole of 1858 I devoted to polishing my work, but it was in 1859, if I'm not mistaken, that I published it in *Otechestvenniye Zapiski* in four instalments in the January, February, March and April issues. Its success exceeded my expectations. And Turgenev once remarked to me briefly: "As long as there is a single Russian left alive, *Oblomov* will be remembered." On another occasion, when I was reading to him the last chapters, which I had written in St Petersburg, he rose quickly from the divan where he was sitting and went to his bedroom, and said, wiping away his tears: "I'm now an old stager, but you've moved me to tears!" (In passing, I would like to point out that these moving words, which touched me to the quick, turned up in Auerbach's novel, *The Country House on the Rhine*,* almost verbatim.) I should point out that throughout this time, from 1855 to 1859, Turgenev was continuing to write his miniatures, *Memoirs of a Hunter*, and, I believe, his novellas 'Asya', 'Faust' and 'Mumu', among others – and all of them, for the most part, charmingly narrated and adorned with interesting and at times poetic details, for example the description of the Rhine in 'Asya', among others. But everyone, both the public and the literary world, was expecting something major and substantial! But "major" was not in his repertoire, and could not have been. He could not establish a literary identity of his own. Such was his talent! He once ruefully confessed this to Pisemsky* and me. "I lack something that you both possess: types, characters – or, in other words, flesh and blood." The reason for this is that he never creates anything on a large scale. (And why? If only he had continued to follow his own path, surely the sum total of his output of miniatures would have constituted a major whole!) He suffered from kidney trouble, which he appears to have contracted in the Paris climate.* Later he complained of gout. In actual fact he possessed no brush: it was all pencils, silhouettes, sketches – all successful and true to life. And the closer his work was to the life and the rural nature of central Russia and that of the minor gentry and the peasantry, the livelier, clearer and warmer were his writings! In this genre he was an extraordinary artist, because he was describing what he loved and knew at first hand. Everywhere else, he does not so much as create or compose: it is as if what he is doing is simply transcribing what he has heard (and this is the truth, as we shall see later on). And all his leading characters, male and female, in what are said to be his major stories – unless (for example Fenechka in *Fathers and Children*) they were taken by him from the real countryside – are pallid and somehow incomplete, and something is missing, as if they were not so much created by him, but rather reflected onto his canvas by some mirror in the vicinity. And that's the way it is! As I have said, he paid close attention to what I said, and was always keen to engage me in conversation and correspondence, and I began to notice that some of my actual words would somehow flash by in one of his stories. Furthermore, I once read in one of his stories, I don't remember which one, a short passage from *Oblomov*, where Oblomov is sitting in the park waiting for Olga and looking around him and enjoying the sight and fragrance of the life and nature surrounding him – the trees, the grass, the butterflies dancing around close together in pairs and the buzzing of the bees... you know the kind of thing: a picture in itself. But I wasn't paying much attention and thought he was better disposed towards me than anyone else. I just thought it was strange that he would be in need of such petty details. Like everyone else, I felt that he was more talented, resourceful and productive than he actually was. This explained his friendliness and cultivation of me, as I now realize! Once, in the autumn of, I believe, the same year I was preparing to publish *Oblomov*, Turgenev came to see me, either from the countryside or from abroad – I'm not sure which – and brought with him a new short novel, *A Nest of the Gentry*, which he had written for the *Sovremennik*. He had rented a flat on Bolshaya Konyushennaya, at Weber's house in the courtyard. Everyone was expecting him to give a reading of his novel, but he claimed to be suffering from bronchitis and was unable to give the reading himself. So Annenkov volunteered to do the reading. A date was set; I heard that Turgenev had invited eight or nine people to dinner, to be followed by a reading. I myself had heard nothing at all from him about the reading or the dinner. I didn't go to the dinner, but afterwards I set out for his flat, since we all felt free to drop in on each other, and didn't have the slightest hesitation in attending the reading later in the evening. The moment I entered, everyone pounced on me to ask why I had not come to the dinner: everyone knew how close Turgenev and I were! I replied that no matter how close two friends might be, when some people are invited and others not, those others should not barge in. "I wasn't invited, so I didn't come," I said. You wouldn't believe how astonished Ivan Sergeych* looked – what an innocent expression there was on his face when he looked at me and mumbled, "What do you mean? Of course I invited you!"

"No you didn't!" I replied with conviction.

He didn't repeat his denial, and soon Annenkov began to read. Everyone knows *A Nest of the Gentry*, although, of course, it's no longer a best-seller – but at the time it was a big hit. But what was it I heard? Exactly what I had been repeating to Turgenev for three years – that is, precisely a compressed but still substantial version of *Malinovka Heights* (or *The Artist*, which was the original title I had planned for the novel.) The idea for the basis of the novel had been taken precisely from the chapter on Raisky's forebears to which I referred earlier, and it was from this canvas that the best parts had been taken and used, although compressed and shortened, and, to put it briefly, the very sap of the novel had been drained and distilled and reproduced in a reformulated and streamlined form. My "Granny" had become his "Auntie"; my "two sisters" had become his "two nieces"; Lavretsky had become an altered version of my Raisky, and also spent nights talking to a friend of his youth, like Raisky with Kozlov. There were the same rendezvous in the garden, *inter alia*. Of course, I wasn't able to supply to him in words the whole fickle, unstable, artistic nature of Raisky, which he shared between Lavretsky and Panshin. Nor did he overlook the figure of the German – my Granny takes out an old book, and in his version the old book is already there on stage. In short, he took a cast of the whole novel, and since portraiture is beyond him, he didn't want to bother with it: he truncated the novel and didn't see it through to a conclusion. My Vera, a True Believer, became his "religious" Liza: he didn't know what to do with her, so he shut her up in a nunnery. Afterwards Annenkov told him that he failed to see the source of her religiosity, so Turgenev added the character of a religious nanny. The miniaturist didn't have the stamina to create a broad vista of life, so all he did was to divide the whole structure into parts, pavilions, summer houses, grottoes and gave them names: "*Ma Solitude*", "*Mon Repos*", "*Mon Hermitage*"* – namely, *A Nest of the Gentry*, *Fathers and Children*, *On the Eve*, *Smoke*... But more of this later. I don't want to get ahead of myself.

The reading had ended. I understood why Turgenev hadn't invited me to dinner. He had hoped I wouldn't turn up that evening for the reading, thinking that afterwards, when something's published, "You can say whatever you like!" I knew that he would feel uneasy trying to watch me while he was reading. Those present started to pass judgement, air opinions and, of course, pay compliments. The whole circle was present: Nekrasov, Panayev, Botkin, Yazykov, Maslov, Tyutchev and, I believe, Count Leo Tolstoy. I waited until everyone had left and I was left alone with Turgenev. I too should have left without saying a word and forgetting about the novel entirely. But that novel was my whole life, and I had invested in it a part of myself, people close to me, my country, the Volga, my home and, I think I can say, the life around me.

When I was describing the novel to Turgenev, I pointed out that after completing *Oblomov* and my current novel, *Raisky*, that would be the end for me and I would have finished all that I had been destined to do, and would write no more. My, how attentively he listened and committed my words to memory! And I should have left without saying a word and thrown away my pen for ever if I had known everything that lay ahead and what happened next and was still going on! I stayed behind and told Turgenev to his face that the novel that had been read was nothing but a copy of my work. How pale he suddenly turned! White like a circus clown, squirming and babbling! "What are you talking about? You don't mean it! I'm throwing it in the fire!" Every word he uttered, every movement he made was a confession that no lie could hide. "No, don't throw it in the fire!" I told him. "I gave it to you. I can do something else. I have a lot in reserve!" I left without further ado. I saw Dudyshkin, who, I believe, had also attended the reading. He laughed when he heard the first words. "Yes, it was very clever of him to glean what he did from your story!" I regretted, of course, that I had been so trusting, but I didn't want to give the matter any importance, and I decided to leave out of my plan the whole chapter about Raisky's forebears. And I did. My relations with Turgenev were strained. We met more than once and had it out. I pointed out to him all his borrowings, and he denied everything. Finally he agreed to give me a letter in which he intended to record everything he had heard from me, namely to summarize everything I had read to him from my novel. I remained indifferent to this proposal, but he was insistent about giving me this letter. He came to see me and sat down to write, and then read out what he had written. He began: "As a matter of fact, I myself at the very beginning noticed the resemblance, influenced most probably by what you had told me about your novel, and subsequently was quick to see a difference." (This letter is lying about somewhere in my house, but as I saw later, it was something that he needed more than I did. The lines I had brought back with me which fully reflected the sense are not totally identical with the original – but it takes a long time to find letters.) And after this introduction he started explaining the difference. In the circumstances, there is of course a difference: I have the Volga, he has some other place; I have Raisky, he has Panshin, a dilettante, I have a "Granny", he has an "Auntie", and he found much of the same kind. When I asked him why he hadn't put anything in his letter about Vera's fall from grace (in my plan I had intended to call her Yelena) or the scenes between her and Granny, he was tongue-tied, it was clearly something he preferred not to discuss – because of some future considerations. But there was no help for it, and he had to respond. He mentioned Kozlov, the teacher, his education, his marriage to the housekeeper's daughter, Ulinka's character – but as to her relationship with her husband, not a word about that. He gave me that letter and I put it in a drawer – and that was that. We continued to meet, but not too cordially.

A Nest of the Gentry was finally published and was a great success, immediately placing its author on a lofty pedestal, because it was published soon after my story and was more meaty, more complex and colourful than anything he had written before or since. "Now I'm a celebrity – the talk of the town!" He was unable to contain himself, even in my presence. He was here, there and everywhere. Everyone sought his company, and he flattered everyone, and charmed them with his amiability and openness, and welcomed the attentions of all and sundry. He never imposed on people, and attracted a loyal following. He was at home to visitors at any time, feeding them unstintingly, and accepted all the invitations that flooded in. He cultivated a clientele of his own, always ready and willing to run errands for him and to be at his beck and call. He now had a cohort of obliging friends: Tyutchev, Maslov and, above all, Annenkov. He was the kind of character in the old comedies and tragedies who was called a "confidant". He was no fool and well educated, fond of literature, and was a bosom pal of the brightest stars in the firmament. He had been a close friend of Gogol,* who called him "Jules". After Gogol died, Annenkov decided that Turgenev was of sufficient eminence to attach himself to him. Turgenev had a way of fawning on his followers and getting them to do him favours at the drop of a hat. After 1855, it could be said that he gradually spent more and more time out of Russia, and wherever he happened to be, he would issue commands to his friends, most of all to Annenkov. "Send me this, find out about that, order that other thing," he would write, signing off with "I press your hand!" Someone who had seen one of these letters said that it contained fourteen instructions listed in order: 1, 2, 3, 4, etc. My behaviour was the polar opposite. For literary purposes I frequented the circle, but for the most part, and in a spirit of total non-conformity, had nothing in common and had nothing to do with them. Religious and other differences in outlook prevented me from forming closer ties with them. It was with Belinsky that I had most in common, principally with his sound critical principles and views on literature, as well as his feeling for works of art and especially for his honesty and rigorous scrupulousness. But what struck me – and at times saddened me – was the incomprehensible speed and ease with which he changed his views or feelings about something or other: he was ready to do so at the drop of a hat. In a word, what frightened me was his impressionability, the way he would turn in whatever direction the wind was blowing and change his mind about anything – be it politics, science or literature. It was frightening. Yet he was admirable, and as sincere, honest and good-natured as could be. I repeat that temperamentally I never felt I really belonged in that whole circle: for that I would have needed to make a sea change and give more of myself than was possible. At the time I was thirty-five or thirty-six, so that although I developed aesthetically in that circle, in all other respects I remained true to the principles of my upbringing. In the evenings I would go to see one or other member of the circle. I lived a cold, solitary existence, but enjoyed being accepted by them, and by people in general, but because of my deep-seated shyness, I shunned intimacy with others, except for the family of the good-natured Mikhail Yazykov, where I was treated as one of them and where I in turn felt at home. I came to realize that literature itself was not sufficient to create meaningful bonds between people, and that, if anything, it might well come between them. There was great camaraderie, it is true, an exchange of ideas and a sharing of tastes, but the problem was that it was precisely the process of getting to know one another which poisoned the sincerity of relationships. Almost all had differences in outlook, and if friendships were in fact formed, it was certainly not on account of shared tastes in literature. Belinsky alone was on friendly terms with everyone, because they held him in unconditional respect. The friendship between Panayev and Botkin, however, had absolutely nothing to do with literature. They liked to share jokes and hang around together, and that was the secret of the strong bonds between them – and the same goes for Druzhinin and Grigorovich. I was able to feel an attachment to Belinsky because of his belief in my talent, as well as his sincerity and straightforwardness. But there was no guarantee that it would last very long. Now, I could also have become attached to Turgenev, but having successfully assessed his character I had become convinced that he was by nature profoundly and chronically a fraud. You might contend that they were all on good terms with one another, and that there was mutual respect among them and they enjoyed chatting among themselves, but you couldn't call it "friendship". I can only repeat that literature, far from promoting friendship among people, actually makes enemies of them, and that there was no love lost between Turgenev and his hangers-on. His friendship tickled their self-esteem, and he made use of them. "What do you think of Annenkov?" I once asked Turgenev, since I didn't know him very well: I found him rather cold and felt ill at ease with him. "In actual fact, Annenkov has his uses, especially when you need to let him loose like a bulldog on an adversary." This, mark you, is what Turgenev said about one of his best friends, supporters and confidants. Regarding another friend, he was even more eloquent at a moment of candour. "If I want to write a story," he once told me, "and portray a typical blockhead – for instance someone like Nikolai

Nikolayevich Tyutchev..." Conversations like this took place before we fell out, of course. And, mind you, Tyutchev would put himself out for him as if he were a saint – and still does! We continued, as I said, to see each other, and he once said to me that he intended to write a novella, and told me what it was about. It was a continuation of that same theme from *Malinovka Heights* – that is to say, the ultimate and tragic fate of Vera. I pointed out to him, of course, that I knew what he was up to: little by little he was borrowing the entire story of Raisky divided into episodes, repeating what he had done in the case of *A Nest of the Gentry*, just changing the background, the setting and the names of the characters and mixing them up somewhat, while leaving intact the plot, the characters and even their motivations, and simply following in my footsteps – at least in one sense, but not in another. In any case, his goal was attained in the following way. While I was still putting the finishing touches to my novel, he had already beaten me to it, thus creating the impression that it was I following in his footsteps... that it was I imitating him! That was what happened, and the effects are still being felt! The plot, like a great net, was flung far and wide. Turgenev displayed a genius for intrigue, and in another career, one with loftier, patriotic goals, he could easily have been another Richelieu or Metternich,* but with his sneaky, selfish aims he is nothing but a literary guttersnipe. The members of our circle knew about our original falling out, talked about it and then fell silent. And I too, of course, kept silent, because it would have been ridiculous to protest about a novel already published and printed when my own novel was still *en herbe,* in the planning stage, and known only to a small circle! This latest example of Turgenev's treachery infuriated me, and I mentioned it first of all to Dudyshkin, whom I had met through the Maykovs before either of us had become writers. Dudyshkin found it funny and strange to see how pale and embarrassed Turgenev looked when in his presence, and in the company of others I made a point of mentioning *A Nest of the Gentry* and also the new short novel while exchanging looks with Dudyshkin.

This might well have gone on *ad infinitum*, but it was Dudyshkin himself who tactlessly blurted it all out into the open. He had a penchant for egging people on when the stage was set for a row, and it amused him to see the parties concerned get heated and make a scene. He got a kick out of it, and he liked nothing more than to add fuel to the fire. This is by no means an admirable trait, but he would seize the slightest opportunity, mostly for the sheer fun of it. But on this occasion it was a bad joke, and almost ended badly. The new novel – a continuation of the Raisky theme – came out with the title *On the Eve*, but I never read it in print: I just knew the version told to me by Turgenev. Dudyshkin and I continued to share a laugh, and Turgenev continued to be embarrassed by all the hints and allusions. Once I met Dudyshkin on the Nevsky Prospekt and asked him where he was going. "To the Velvet Cheat" – which is what we called him privately – "for dinner."

"You will be dining at my expense!" I joked (meaning, of course, my honorarium for the novel *On the Eve*).

"Shall I tell him?" said Dudyshkin to tease me.

"Yes, tell him, tell him!" I replied in the same spirit, and then we parted.

Who would have thought that Dudyshkin would actually tell him? And he did, even in the presence of five or six others. He was hoping, of course, to embarrass Turgenev again, something he would have enjoyed. Turgenev had his back to the wall. He had to choose between confessing – something he would never do – or defend himself. Annenkov, his pal, supporter and confidant, appeared on the stage, of course.

The next day they both called on me, but, finding me out, left me a note with the question: what was the meaning of the words which Dudyshkin had passed on to them? I went to see Dudyshkin and showed him the note. I asked him myself to explain the meaning of the note.

"Well, it was you who told me to tell him what you said yesterday," he pointed out timidly. "You couldn't have meant it seriously…"

"And if I had asked you to hit him, would you have done it?" I asked him, and Dudyshkin understood how unpardonably stupid he had been.

He was a well-meaning, straightforward person, highly intelligent in his own special way, cautious and hard to categorize – and yet here he had gone too far, carried away by his urge to tease people. He suffered bouts of jaundice and had visibly yellowed and lost weight. All I told him was that if it ended badly – in a duel, for example – then I reserved the right to count on him as my second. He agreed, but took the note from me, and said that he would see Turgenev and give him an answer both on his own behalf and mine, and without detriment to me. I told him only that I would stand by what I had said. I may have forgotten what he said, but remembered only that the two parties would settle the matter once and for all in the presence of witnesses.

Apart from Annenkov and Dudyshkin, Druzhinin and Nikitenko* were also present. The proceedings took place in my home. But, of course, nothing came of it. The novel, for the most part, had been recounted in private, then in the presence of Dudyshkin; parts of it had been told to Druzhinin. Dudyshkin and Druzhinin were not much interested in the plan of the novel, and knew only its outline, therefore they could neither approve nor refute anything. Nikitenko was invited as a guest of honour and witness, known as he was as a mild-mannered person. Annenkov was a crony of Turgenev, and as a matter of course always sided with him no matter what, because of his pride in the association. And Dudyshkin, who was the cause of all this trouble, was more put out than either of the two of us – Turgenev and myself. At first, Turgenev became very pale and turned red. He was afraid that I would mount a vigorous defence, possessing, as I did, all the necessary evidence and being able to introduce it in the proper order, stating all the positions which had been taken, shared or changed. But I was just as embarrassed as Turgenev, and was unhappy with the whole story. He of course demanded solid proof, which did not exist except for my own hopelessly outdated plan, which I alone could make sense of.

When we had taken our seats, we began by relating the circumstances of our first disagreement. This was followed by a reading of the letter which I had been forced to write, which contained references to a few parts of my novel but overlooked the fact that he wanted to appropriate them. It was here that Turgenev gave a sample of that ability to put on an act which has always been his trademark. It was something which is nothing more or less than a series of artificial, carefully pondered set pieces. I believe that even when he is alone at home he was incapable of sitting down or standing up spontaneously, without ulterior motives and in total sincerity. Never! So it was in this case, where he acted out his carefully planned script, taking in everyone except me and Dudyshkin, who knew him through and through, and would always tell me in advance: "I'm looking forward to watching him lie."

"To betray the trust of a friend!" Turgenev would exclaim – and I, disheartened by this depressing scene, would feebly and in a few words say what a lot I saw that we had in common, and in spite of myself go into detail about all the trivial memories we shared but were tedious for outsiders. I was aware that to all these indifferent listeners it was of no interest, and that there was no way I could entertain them with these banalities.

Druzhinin and Nikitenko did their best to smooth things over with such generalities as "You are both worthy and talented persons, and, as it were, have happened to come up with similar plots: one of you represents the same thing in a certain way and the other in a different way", and so on. Turgenev was at pains to emphasize the similarities in his story *On the Eve*, and finally said that I probably had not read it. That was true, but I did remember his account of it. "You should definitely read it!" he insisted, and I promised to. In connection with this short novel, he tried a crude and ludicrous trick. The heroine in his story is called Yelena, and in my plan, instead of Vera , her name had been Yelena. "If I had wanted to borrow it, I would surely have changed the name!" he said, and looked more cheerful. Annenkov also perked up, seeing that his pal and protector was getting away with it. I kept silent in the face of such shamelessness, since I had clearly forfeited any chance of establishing the truth, and once again regretted that I hadn't given up right at the start. We all stood up.

"Goodbye," I said. "Thank you all, gentlemen, for your attention."

Turgenev was the first to pick up his hat; his face had shed any sign of his previous pallor and embarrassment, and was now a healthy pink, a sign of his satisfaction at the fact that I hadn't been able to prove his *plagiat**– the word he had used rather than using its Russian equivalent (*et pour cause*).*

"Goodbye, Ivan Alexandrovich," he said, making a grand exit. "This is our last meeting."

At which, Dudyshkin too raised his head more boldly, now that it had all ended uneventfully.

* * *

So several years went by without our meeting or greeting, and my existence became even more solitary. Afterwards I took a look at *On The Eve*, and saw that there really wasn't that much similarity! But in print I hardly recognized it. It was not at all the same story that I had heard read. The basic plot was the same, but many details were missing, and the whole setting had been radically altered. The protagonist was some Bulgarian.* It was simply not the same story. The fact was that when he was recounting it to me, he was testing me to see whether I knew what had become of Vera and Volokhov, and when he had seen that I had grasped the plot, he changed a great deal in the printed version – something for which he was extremely gifted! He continued to behave in the same way, systematically, borrowing from me, as we shall see, but changing the setting and the locations, and retaining the main characters, but changing their names, nationalities and so on.

However, I continued with my novel.* In 1860 and 1861 I published extracts from "The Grandmother", "The Portrait" and "Belovodova" in the *Sovremennik* and in *Otechestvenniye*

Zapiski. I continued, in my naivety, with my readings and discussions (not, of course, with Turgenev, whom I was not seeing any more, but with Druzhinin, Botkin and others) about what I was doing. Turgenev knew all about this. Several years went by – up to the death of Druzhinin in, I think, 1864. In the summer, I took time off from my job, and continued to work on my novel – sluggishly, slowly, just a few chapters at a time – but in St Petersburg, under grey skies and often in bad weather, I couldn't get any work done. In the church at the funeral of Druzhinin at the Smolensk Cemetery, Annenkov suddenly came up to me and told me that Turgenev wanted to shake hands with me, and asked me what I would say to that. "I will offer him my hand," I replied, and we made up as if nothing had come between us. We started meeting again, talking, dining together – I had forgotten everything. I never exchanged a word with him about my novel, and just mentioned briefly that I was continuing to write – in the summer, when I was taking the waters. Turgenev's main motive in wishing to put our quarrel behind us (a quarrel which had become public knowledge after our "meeting in the presence of witnesses") was, as I was to realize later, to erase the memory of my accusation that he had stolen or plagiarized – as he was careful to put it – parts of my work. In the second place, he was anxious to be able to follow my activities at closer quarters and hinder the completion of my novel, from which he had appropriated his *Fathers and Children* and *Smoke*, and pre-empt me in literary circles both at home and abroad to prevent the revelation of his weakness and the true source of his writings. In order to allay suspicion, he would from time to time come out with works of his own, very pretty, although rather threadbare stories, such as 'Asya' and 'First Love'. In me he saw his only rival in his own particular literary field. Leo Tolstoy had only just begun his war stories. Grigorovich specialized in stories of peasant life. Pisemsky and Ostrovsky* came later. In effect, I was the only one standing in his way, and he made it his business to tear me to pieces, to thwart me – including abroad in literary and bookselling circles – and by his own negative propaganda to prevent my name becoming known. In those circles he was trusted, since he alone was known personally – and that was the secret of his success. He had prepared a plan: he assumed the role of a genius, the star of the new literary period, and prospered and is still successfully acting the part. In the summer, I travelled twice from Marienbad to Baden-Baden, where Turgenev was living, near the Viardot family.* I did some writing there, but didn't show or mention anything to Turgenev. Just once for some reason or another I let slip something by saying: "You remember, in my novel—" He didn't let me finish; his expression changed and he mumbled something quickly: "No, I don't remember anything – nothing!" He had so *brusquement** interrupted me that I was stopped in my tracks and just stood there looking at him. He was all pale, and looked away from me. I had given up ever starting a conversation with him. At the time he was reading to me something by Feoktistov,* something like *The Brigadier*.* By now I had given up mentioning anything about my work. However, before then his two short novels, *Fathers and Children* and *Smoke*, had been published. Then, a long time later, I read them both, and saw that the content, the themes and the characters were drawn from the same source – *Malinovka Heights* – and in *Smoke* it was just the notion of "smoke" (my "Mirage", Part Two, Chapter 20, *Malinovka Heights*).

He is a master of forgery and parallels. He skims the general idea like the cream off the milk, as is the case with the relations between the old and new generations – since his images do not embody the idea so much as suggest it in the titles. Take *Fathers and Children*, for example. The paucity of content and invention prevent him from treading his own path. So that even in *Fathers and Children*, for example, he imitated even the skeleton plan of *Malinovka Heights* (as in the case of Raisky and Volokhov), where his new characters travel to a provincial town – and he did it again in *A Nest of the Gentry*, where he introduces, like in *Malinovka Heights*, the character of the old woman: my "Granny" and his "Auntie". The same goes for the two female characters (Vera and

Marfenka): Odintsova and Fenechka are distant versions of Vera and Marfenka, from a different background. But by repeating twice one and the same old woman, for all his trying, he failed to capture my "Granny" with his old woman. He had leapt many years ahead, but when *Malinovka Heights* came out, I was very pleased with "Granny's" reception, while his old ladies made no impression at all. This was understandable: what he had written was not an offspring to which he himself had given birth and raised, but a fictional emanation without flesh and blood.

Here, however, I must pay tribute to his sensitive powers of observation; to his credit is his creation of the figure of Bazarov in *Fathers and Children*. At the time he was writing this story, nihilism had barely raised its head, except perhaps in theory, like the first sliver of a new moon, but the author had enough intuition to see it as a phenomenon, and it was within his power, such as it was, to portray this original character in complete and exhaustive form. For me in the Sixties it was easier to create the character Volokhov on the basis of the rise of numerous apostles of nihilism, both in St Petersburg and in the provinces. His aim was firstly to diminish my reputation, and secondly to make himself the leading figure in Russian literature and make a name for himself abroad. In essence, he was aiming at occupying the place that had once been occupied by Pushkin, Lermontov and Gogol – that is to say to succeed them in their role, but without their genius, creativity, imagination and profundity. His undeniable talent as a miniaturist and extraordinary feline agility helped him to a certain extent – with the assistance and goodwill of someone else, namely myself – to create the aspiring foremost writer and the would-be leader of a new school of literary realism. It is a pose he adopts particularly when he is abroad. I don't know whether he will ultimately succeed.

To continue. I have never said anything to him about *Fathers and Children* and *Smoke*. I had praised the former, and I had read the latter only in December last year (1875) when I discovered in it the theme of my *Malinovka Heights*, as mentioned above, where fantasy had been reduced to smoke. This *Smoke* as a work of art is negligible. It seems that there is not a single outstanding character, nor the slightest suggestion of an artist in it. It is a caricature of Russian society; it is a distortion of the true image of Russian life and semi-activity. Here he has borrowed what I happened to have said on the passage I have mentioned (Part Two, Chapter 20) of *Malinovka Heights*, and furthermore went so far as to include little gems (in the dialogue between Potugin and Litvinov) extracted from the conversation I had put into the mouths of Raisky and Volokhov late at night as they were drinking punch (Chapter 15 in the same part). All of this has been borrowed and wasted so that he can claim the authorship of these ideas – somehow implying it is others who have done the borrowing! This explain his barrenness, his lack of a spark of creativity, especially in *Smoke*, which is virtually unreadable – so dull, long-winded and flaccid – being, as it is, nothing but a rehashing of the work of others.

To throw people off the scent, he has set all the action in foreign countries – another one of his evasive tactics! His goal and method has always focused primarily on plundering all my ideas, and approximating his characters as close as possible to mine, purloining the best scenes, and even actual language and then putting together the pieces the way children do when they make toy theatres out of cardboard, placing the left wings on the right and vice versa – treachery! For example, turning my male characters into females or vice versa, and so on. If a "similarity" was pointed out to him, he would protest (as he explained in his explanation regarding *A Nest of the Gentry* and *On the Eve*) that "my character was a doctor, and his was a teacher" or "it was my male character who was the jealous one, and not the female" – or the other way round. And when my novel was published, he would sneakily point out various examples of "similarity" to his cronies. And even when he didn't, readers would somehow vaguely recall, "I've seen this before – in Turgenev, I think!" If you were to read both in succession, similarities might not strike you, in both cases, because of stylistic differences: my diffuseness and his brevity and compression, since he needs to prune, to squeeze out the juice, to rearrange, and thus create the impression that it was his own work. He showed the same ability, incidentally, by distorting my first novel *The Same Old Story*, published a long time ago in the *Sovremennik* (in 1847).

I believe it was in 1870 or 1871 that a major work by Turgenev, *Torrents of Spring*,* was published in *Vestnik Evropy*.* No one except me noticed that it was nothing but a rehash of the first part of *The Same Old Story*. At first glance it is not noticeable, but if the two were compared (which, of course, it never occurred to anyone to do), the similarities could not be missed. To perpetrate this stunt more effectively and anonymously, he had the action take place in Frankfurt, thus totally distorting the setting. But if you analysed it bit by bit, you would find that everything is to be found in my work. To start with, the central idea of the first part of *The Same Old Story* is all there: first love, sincere, youthful tears, like those of the young Aduyev, betrayal, a cooling off by one of the parties, and suffering on the part of the other. The character of the positive uncle (in my version) is in his version allotted to the solid and practical (like Aduyev's uncle) German. It also contains an aborted duel, another love story, following on the heels of the first, and many other details – not forgetting the berries which were being washed by my Nadenka, as well as his protagonist.* The most important scene, the heart of the novel, was a horse-riding scene with, in my version, Nadenka and the count, and in his a lioness of a coquette with his protagonist (whose name I have forgotten). To avert suspicion he gave the role of my Nadenka (the unfaithful one) to a man, and the role of Aduyev to a young woman. In place of my (frankly feeble) Tafayeva, he portrayed, very successfully, a flirtatious lady with a clodhopper of a husband. Then he covered up his imitation with boring and fuzzy details. Granted, such a wholesale make-over could only be attempted by a talented writer with his particular skills. In my version, the horse-riding scene is purely incidental and merges naturally with the other scenes. He on the other hand emphasized this scene, and gave it such prominence with all the finesse of a miniaturist, but to a point where it verged on vulgarity. Finishing touches of this kind are possible only in the case of miniatures, but he attaches great importance to them, while, so I have heard, he refers to my writings as "raw material".

You see, he took it upon himself to correct and put the finishing touches on my work. In my case, because of the variety of pictures and scenes, the result would appear too finicky and meticulous and reduce major figures and buildings to the scale of toys. As to him, he is so lacking in the ability to discern the essence and fundamentals of life that he is incapable of grasping phenomena of any complexity or taking a comprehensive view of life. He has great powers of observation and sensitivity, but little imagination, and cannot wield a brush, except perhaps to produce the simplest pictures, miniature landscapes and straightforward silhouettes of two-dimensional people. That is why he has to borrow the settings and frameworks of others, and follow in their footsteps.

He tried to spoil Shakespeare, but failed even at that. What he produced were caricatures – for example *A King Lear of the Steppes*. Why tinker with great things only to fashion from manure the ugliest and most disgusting figures? Is it permissible to make a mockery of such a tragic and colossal figure as King Lear and use it as a label for the absurd figure of a filthy and shabby creature from some backwater, notable only for being able to "shift a billiard table with his belly, to swallow three chamber pots full of porridge and emit a foul smell"?! Is it possible to stoop so low as to take such a great model as Lear, bequeathed to mankind, and chuck it onto a pile of filth? But Shakespeare emerged as unscathed as a bronze statue of him would if some kid had thrown a pebble at it. You can't steal it. That 'Hamlet of the Shchigrovsky District'...* just another nonentity: how can these figures be compared with his manikins cut out from paper! If you want to be taken for someone else, then stand on tiptoe, leap ahead and take a peep over his shoulder at what he has written – you can no doubt blind people, cheat, rob and slander them and appropriate what belongs to others! Turgenev wrote *Torrents of Spring* – plagiarized from *The Same Old Story* – when there was nothing more to steal from me. Clearly this was something he did in order to expand his reputation abroad. If he happened to be living in Paris and was in touch with writers and booksellers there, and it had somehow escaped his notice that something that I had written had been translated into French, he would immediately made a point of mentioning *Torrents of Spring* and telling people: "Oh, I had already written this. The same plan, the same characters, the best parts... the author is imitating me!" And he really knew what he was doing! Who on earth would take the trouble to find out that my story had been written twenty-five years before his, when I had never even set eyes on him? And, in any case, who is going to check or research similarities or repetitions of the same scenes? No one! Readers will just say that on this or that subject something has already been written by Turgenev, "the Russian genius, *chef de la nouvelle école, comme romancier*".*

He carved out a permanent niche for himself in Berlin too, where he had been a student, forged literary connections (with Auerbach and others) and quietly made his way, whispering and influencing public opinion in favour of Russian writers. Through influential friends he got himself translated into a number of languages, and was clever enough to see to it that nothing of his was translated which cast a shadow on, or was damaging to, his reputation. But at the same time, in order to allay suspicion or envy, he promoted translations of the earlier celebrities – Pushkin, Gogol, Lermontov – or those of newer authors who didn't rival him. When *Oblomov* was published, I received acknowledgments from all quarters, and received from abroad two requests to permit translations *avec l'autorisation de l'auteur*.* In my naivety, I sent a letter asking Turgenev to write and tell them that they could go ahead and do what they wanted. He seized on the letter eagerly and said: "Very well, I will!" And a long time later, without showing me any answer, he somehow suggested that he had approached some bookseller, and (so he said) uttered the following phrase:

"*Je ne doute pas de leur parfaite honorabilité*"* – and words to that effect. And what happened I still have no idea even now. Probably he refused on my behalf – anyway, that was how it ended up. Otherwise there would have been no point in even using these words. I have always been indifferent to these translations, and when I have been asked for permission, I have responded that I'd rather not be translated, but do whatever you want, I won't sue you! However, translating me into French, especially if it were done quickly, would foil Turgenev, and would unmask his feeble attempt at forgery, and in particular would prevent him from passing on what he himself has not copied from *Malinovka Heights* to other writers such as Flaubert,* for example, and Auerbach. "It's improbable, like a fairy tale," people will perhaps say in response to this. Improbable indeed, but true. How much that's improbable actually happens in this world, how many lies masquerade as the truth! This is my analysis of this affair, and it explains the long-drawn-out torment I have suffered.

Falsehood and vanity are deep-seated elements of Turgenev's personality. What is known as a heart is something which he simply does not possess, and that's why there isn't a shred of sincerity within him. He is highly intelligent, but his mind is not that powerful human faculty which assesses, judges and weighs events within a whole context, and thus makes sound and correct decisions as a faculty of a far-sighted and acute vision which is capable of reaching the right conclusions. This power does not lie: it may err in terms of trivial details, but never loses sight of the general direction and ultimate goal – it has no need to lie! I would even claim that a true and principled intelligence is at work only when the person and the intelligence and the heart are working in unison. But his kind of intelligence, subtle and flexible and wily, is on the lookout for loopholes and roundabout routes regardless of and even scorning commonly accepted norms of conduct, blindly placing his trust in the strength of his underhand and cunning calculations. His favourite tool has always been his constant and inherent insincerity, which he wields so skilfully. He has always worn it at his belt like one of those mounted riders from the mountains. He lies desperately, crazily, even passionately, carried away in his blindness. His ability to fabricate, not only in his books, but also in his words, has been amazing, while his shiftiness and barefaced denial is even more so. When you tell him, for example, "Ivan Sergeyevich, you said this or that" – and he is bound to deny it – he will look astounded and disavow it, and if you persist, he will say: "I swear to God in all honesty I never said it!" And he will place his hand on his heart and burst into laughter as if shocked by such an insinuation. Onlookers, of course, are bewildered, especially his supporters and hangers-on, who usually end up believing him. "I mean, how could Turgenev..." they say, and then turn on his opponent. But if, with his canine sensitivity, he sniffs the possibility that some enterprise may not turn out well for him and he might be unmasked, he pre-empts the opposition, in case he runs into people he knows, by arming himself with a well-thought-out, natural-seeming explanation – and he gets away with it! Dissembling and putting on an act have become second nature to him, as is his hail-fellow-well-met manner along with his feigned absent-mindedness, as someone afflicted by occasional bouts of melancholy – a most unlikely diagnosis in his particular case: this "melancholy" is the sleepiness of a fox. He put on a front of someone not especially interested in anything in particular: even literature was something that he only dabbled in casually. He kept silent, but was always watching and listening, and nothing escaped his attention. What made it easier to fool others was his strapping build, his handsome head, his attractive streaks of grey hair and venerable beard. There was also his thoughtful look and endearing manners. The poison of lies and devious malice was expressed only in a whisper into the ear of one or other of his friends, accompanied by a touch of humour and a benevolent expression, knowing as he did that it would spread and find an enemy while he kept his distance. It is the way cats behave – scratch and hide – leaving only the smell behind! The breed he belongs to is the demure, and to no one is the description "That one is affectionate, but it bites" more applicable – the opposite being the line "The other one is a beast, but gentle".

To what I have said about all that he has "borrowed" from me there may be serious and justifiable objections. Let's say, for example, that he may have "borrowed" events, characters or even typical scenes and settings of my own, if all of this had been told to him according to my detailed plan and in the proper sequence. But how could he have borrowed the exact wording from some other place, if only, for example, the theme of the actual mirage from *Malinovka Heights* (Part Two, Chapter 15) which I have mentioned, and developed an idea which I had compressed in just a few lines in terms of "smoke" and expanded it into a whole story? After all, I hadn't even completed that novel, and was taking a long time to work on it while I was taking the waters abroad – a period of some twenty years which stretched from 1849 to the end of the '60s. Could I really in 1855, while recounting the entire novel, have also recounted the mirages as I had described them in my own work? Would it not in fact have been more natural for me to have taken this idea from his novel, which had been published before *Malinovka Heights*, and included it in my novel? Yes, that is likely. But Turgenev actually turned the whole thing inside out – and getting the jump on me thanks to the forgotten episode of the plagiarism and the confrontation – craftily spread the rumour here, and especially abroad, that he was the leader, but that someone who could "wield a brush with great talent" had imitated him (see *Histoire de la littérature russe* by Courrière).* Here, of course (as I later discovered), was another example of his governing impulse, envy, and he laid the blame at my door. Very clever, but nasty! He has literally borrowed what could be the subtitle of *Woe From Wit** – namely, "that someone who is clever cannot be a rogue". What can I use as proof of the opposite? His clever diplomatic letter? Briefly, his message left out any reference to what he had already purloined and what he still intended to. I have two more notes where he says that he will never forget the details and scenes which I recounted to him

and Dudyshkin from *Oblomov* and *The Artist*. When presented
with these notes, he could say that he might have wanted to pick,
let's say, a general idea or two, two or three characters, a couple
of scenes and motifs – and that's all he remembers. Dudyshkin,
Druzhinin and Botkin, to whom I spoke, are dead. In short, it has
all been carefully thought through, although, I repeat, it's all vile
and petty! And no one is going to be able to offer an independent
opinion – everything has been done in an underhand way, and he
himself has taken advantage of my goodwill and shared it gener-
ously with others, as I shall reveal later. For now I shall respond
to the objections which I anticipate. How, for example, could he
in *Smoke* have made use of a page from a novel which had not
been written to write something of his own? To do this it would
have been necessary to have that page right in front of him. Am
I saying that I was writing a novel without revealing a single
word of it to him? This is how I would answer that question. In
the years between 1860 and 1865 I had completed the first three
parts, and had been reading them out to anyone who cared to
listen. So Turgenev must have had my manuscript right in front
of him in order to make his forgery so similar. It must have been
in his possession. But how? Where? This is very regrettable and
painful for me. I can only offer a partial explanation, because I
myself am not entirely cognizant of all the ins and outs of this
Jesuitical intrigue of which I was the victim. I am saddened and
hurt not just for myself, but also for all those who were in any
way involved in what was going on between Turgenev and myself.
Their part in this whole event was most unsavoury! Turgenev, the
initiator and driving force in this affair, could not have done all
this alone and unaided.

But first I want to give a full account of the part played by
Turgenev himself, before describing how substantially he was
aided and abetted by unexpected allies. Turgenev had been receiving my manuscripts, or at least copies of them. While I was away
taking the waters, I had carelessly left my manuscripts on my
desk or in an unlocked chest. I was absent for quite a long time

and had left the key. Some of my acquaintances, including those who seemed to be on good terms with me, had been listening attentively to my readings and had been carefully taking notes (as I had witnessed myself before finally putting two and two together). Once, a whole group of strangers in Marienbad had taken rooms in the same corridor as mine – at the time I didn't realize why, although I couldn't help being surprised, because of certain fleeting signs, that they were taking an interest in me. I got the feeling that they were following me, and (as I later realized) that they could have been making themselves at home in my room while I was out. I saw that they had arranged for me to run into various people and get into conversation with them in order to worm out of me my opinions of my acquaintances and constantly bringing up the name of Turgenev in the hope of eliciting from me an expression of envy of him. I was placed in a very difficult position by their incessant attempts, prompted and encouraged by Turgenev himself to label me "his jealous rival". I had long since ceased to read Russian novels and stories, having learnt by heart Pushkin, Lermontov and Gogol, and of course could not be a whole-hearted admirer of Turgenev and Dostoevsky, and later Pisemsky, whose talents didn't match those of the first three. It was only the humour and objectivity of Ostrovsky which raised him close to the level of Gogol and thus came close to satisfying me. I read Dostoevsky's *Poor People*, which contained maybe a dozen pages which came alive, but later, when he created characters such as Golyadkin and Prokharchin,* I gave up reading him, except for his excellent *House of the Dead*.* Since then I have read none of his works – not even *Crime and Punishment** – which they say are very good, and that's all. Of Pisemsky's works I am familiar only with *The Carpenters** and what he read aloud to us (he was a lively reader, and even acted some parts very well). If this was because I was just fed up, or perhaps because I had written so much myself, I don't know, but I wasn't reading anything in Russian. If people ask me whether I have been reading anything by anyone of them, the answer is "No". People will say that it's because of envy. Well, if you *do* read something and are too critical, you will be told it is because of envy. And people will look you straight in the eye as they say it – with stupid looks on their faces! In a word, I can't help noticing that I am getting strange looks wherever I go and whatever I say. I was seeing a lot then, but, of course, only came to understand it later when I had become the victim of a vast tragi-comedy of unpleasantness, coarse jokes and sly digs – all so painful to me that I was obliged to resign from my job, abandon writing, turn my back on society and lock myself away in my room. What had once been a healthy and blooming body had now been seriously damaged, and I was losing sleep. My nerves suffered grievously, and I was left extremely depressed and almost went out of my mind. Perhaps, when people hear me talking like this, they will say I am delirious and have made the whole thing up. Oh, if only that were true! Then I would solemnly declare myself out of my mind and suffering from hypochondria. But it's the truth!

Let me now turn to Turgenev. In his short novel *Smoke*, he used the idea of a mirage and put it in the very same setting, once again "borrowing" from *Malinovka Heights*, Parts Two and Three – a straightforward, virtually transparent and word-for-word copy from my novel when he heard me read it. He attached great importance to this novel (*Malinovka*) even when it existed only in embryo. I failed to detect the significance of all this at the time. Only now can I see how much he used for himself and then shared with Auerbach and Flaubert in their parallel novels based on *Malinovka* – only now can I fully realize what a success it might have enjoyed if all of them hadn't beaten me to it with their plagiarized versions! In *Smoke* he purloined from Parts Two and Three some small ideas and scenes (which I had already written), and of course made his protagonists as different as possible. In my version, for example (Part Three, Chapter 2), the characters were having a very scrappy and ill-informed conversation about politics in Granny's drawing room, dominated, incidentally, by General Tychkov. In *Smoke* Turgenev also depicted some contemporary generals, ignorant fops who had no idea what they were talking about. In my Chapter 9* I had a ridiculous character, an aging coquette called Polina Karpovna. He too had one of the same kind – a lady with a yellow hat perched on yellow hair and ridiculously affected. He had a stout general who spoke in exactly the same manner, but not in the same vein as mine – the same conversation about the legal status of the peasantry as my general. He had an Irina in an hotel just like my Vera, contemptuous of everyone and thinking about Litvinov, whereas the other one was thinking of Volokhov. His Tychkov voiced the same views about young people, and even used the same name, Boris (who flirted with the ridiculous and pretentious woman while laughing at her up his sleeve). Turgenev often has recourse to this tactic in order to demonstrate that he wouldn't dream of borrowing (otherwise "I obviously would have changed the names!"). Raisky is called Boris. But he is always casually pointing out to his devoted fans these similarities, not forgetting to mention the names, and claiming that all this has been borrowed from him and included in my novel – and not the other way round. And Litvinov, like Raisky (*Smoke*, Chapter 10), criticizes the generals just as his counterpart criticizes Tychkov; his honest plebeian pride is wounded by their remarks and views. On the basis of my manuscript or a detailed account of it given to him by a member of my audience at a reading, Turgenev embroiders his own handiwork in different tints or hues, and sometimes different colours, or sometimes the places or pages where he puts them, entwining them with his own words – or interpreting my words in his own way. As if robbing my pages were not enough, he also takes actual expressions from *Malinovka Heights* – for example: "We Russians don't have any work" (Part Two, Chapter 20) – in order to purloin this thought and use it as the plot for a story and detaching the last of one of my planned chapters and radically changing the circumstances. He scatters and redistributes the scenes, conversations and expressions that he has "borrowed" from me so bewilderingly that at first I myself fail to identify the places where material has been "borrowed" from me: it is only after I have read a whole passage and have absorbed specific details that I begin to recognize the structure of my whole plan as well as expressions similar to my own popping up here and there in his text, or the very same descriptions and phraseology as my own, but in a different order and mixed with his insertions of his own devising! He can make use ten times over, thanks to his talent and ingenuity, of a Vera or Marfenka, a Raisky or a Volokhov. It was for good reason that Belinsky once said about me in his presence: "His novel *The Same Old Story* contains enough material for a dozen novellas, but he uses it all up for just one novel!" And that is precisely what Turgenev did by mining *Malinovka Heights* for *A Nest of the Gentry*, *Fathers and Children* and *On the Eve*, reprising not only the content and the characters, but also its plan! And from *The Same Old Story* he mined *Torrents of Spring* too! So, with the exception of *Memoirs of a Hunter* and a few of his own stories like 'Asya', 'First Love' and 'Faust', the wellspring of his activity, Turgenev is acting as the leader of a new school in French literature in which he transplanted the whole of Russian literature either directly or by casually conveying to others the content and the very form of Russian writing. It was in *A Nest of the Gentry* that he came closer than in all his other works to *Malinovka Heights*, so that at his readings some members of his audience, so I have heard, have said that it was from there (from *Malinovka*) that something seems to have been borrowed and put in *A Nest of the Gentry*. His other borrowings are so veiled that only he and I see their clear resemblance to *Malinovka*. These are what I call "parallels", where Turgenev, trendy by nature, and one of the "new" men, valued ideas most of all, but not the images by which to express them, putting himself, at the expense of others, as a "thinker" over and above an artist. None of this does he produce out of his own head: he relies exclusively on what I supply, which he calls "raw material", and unabashedly makes use of a topic of mine disguised in images either in the text itself or in the titles (*Fathers and Children*, *Smoke*, etc.) – that is to say, precisely what newspaper columnists do with their eye-catching headlines: "A Row", "A Corpse", "A Shocking Scene in Public", etc. He then goes to develop these items in concoctions built on my ideas or images, as he does in *Smoke*. For example, in the conversations between Potugin and Litvinov in *Smoke*, he depicted the exchanges between Volokhov and Raisky as moralizing. And if you add to this a character or a scene along the lines of *Memoirs of a Hunter*, you get the desired result.

All this, of course, I spotted, and got right to the heart of the matter, later, but not when this was all going on, thanks to the plot of which I was the target and the victim, as I have described above. It was this that made me scrutinize Turgenev and his machinations more closely. Turgenev himself I had already known for a long time, but thought he would be satisfied with *A Nest of the Gentry* and *On the Eve* and leave it at that – which is probably what he would have done left to himself without his supporters. I would go further and say that what has already been written is only the first part, but the more important part lies ahead.

In 1867 and 1868, Count Alexei Konstantinovich Tolstoy (the author of *Ivan The Terrible* and other dramas) and his wife spent the winter here. He was universally popular because of his talent and intelligence, but most of all because of his benevolent, open, straightforward character and unfailing cheerfulness. People were drawn to him like flies, and his home was always crowded with visitors – and because the count was equally friendly and hospitable to everyone, there were people of every stripe, calling and intellectual standing, including the beau monde, in which he had many friends and relatives.

The countess – a refined, intelligent, educated and emancipated woman, a voracious reader in four languages who loved art and was well versed in it and literature – was, in short, one of only few truly educated women. She was, to an extent, a judge and critic of her husband's writing, and he made no secret of the fact that he valued her opinion. We had got to know them earlier in Karlsbad,* where we met every day. I had an open invitation to their home, and visited them almost daily. I was already growing tired of everything, even of literature, and was lazily glancing through my manuscripts – and, having long since completed Part Three of *Malinovka Heights*, I felt like simply giving up on the novel without finishing it.

Once I met Stasyulyevich* there, when he was trying to enliven his learned journal with belles-lettres and follow the example of Tolstoy, who, after *The Death of Ioann** was working on the drama *Fyodor Ioannovich.** I told Tolstoy that I had three parts of the novel *Raisky, the Artist*, but would probably never finish it, and was fed up with it, and was wondering whether it would be all right to leave it as it was, in three parts. All three seized on this idea, and asked me to give them a reading of what I had written. For a whole week, all three of them, the count, the countess and Stasyulyevich, came to see me at 2 p.m. and left at 5 p.m. How astonished they were by these three parts! How much I had grown in their estimation! Although they were restrained in their approval, I sensed a change in their attitude to me, and they could not conceal their surprise, from time to time giving me a look and whispering among themselves. It was clear that I had made an impression on them. For days, Stasyulyevich practically didn't leave my side and came to see me every day – and I promised to place the novel with him.

All this was encouraging, and made me determined to finish the novel during the summer at the spa. But once again I noticed something strange in the count's attitude to me. When he came to listen to me reading my novel, for some reason he found it necessary to hurry to Berlin to see Auerbach, and urged me to leave St Petersburg and go abroad as soon as possible in order, I thought, to prevent me meeting Turgenev, who was expected in St Petersburg. "I wonder why?" I thought at the time, but couldn't fathom it – it was as if I was lost in the woods. What up to then had been nothing but a vague suspicion was becoming a conviction which grew stronger with every passing day. But I was still very far from suspecting the tangled web of intrigue – a joke, really.

I only gradually came to wake up to the idea that Turgenev was spreading lies about me: that he was in fact going around telling people that he had been recounting his stories to me, and that I was envious of him and I was the one who was spreading rumours and slander about him – instead of the other way round – when it was he who was exploiting my goodwill. According to him, he never said anything about me. These denials filtered through to me one way or another. I began to get an inkling of what he was up to by the number of questions people from all quarters were asking me about what I thought of him as a person and as a writer and that kind of thing. The count put the same questions to me, watching me carefully as I answered. I understood what was behind it. Turgenev knew from our first two disagreements that I was not about to disown my own property – including my opinion of him, which will not change – and consequently, even if I have forgotten things in the past and I have, as far as any new deliberate "borrowings" by him from my work are concerned, I will not keep quiet about it.

As for him, after stealing his "similarities", he will naturally refrain from mentioning me for good or ill. After all, when would a thief ever mention his theft? But the victim will, of course, cry thief – unquestionably! Accordingly, it will end up looking as if I am slandering him out of jealousy, since his stories will have been published before my novel, making it appear that I am imitating him and profiting from his reputation – both as a writer and as a man! It's all cleverly calculated! He has whispered all this into the ears of his hangers-on, cronies and lickspittles, and they have contributed their own fabrications and inventions. And why wouldn't you believe him? "Such a talent and such a nice, respectable and straightforward fellow, with a delightful pen, such charm and so good-natured, likeable and irreproachable. In a word, butter wouldn't melt in his mouth." Yes indeed, a lie can be so eloquent and persuasive! And so often can be an effective and useful weapon in the hands of someone who knows how to use it! But it is said that the truth will out and bring down the liar.

But is it true? For if it is not, life is not worth living! However, I have never gone around making a fuss about being robbed: I forgot the old goings-on, especially after we came together over the grave of Druzhinin – and if sometimes it had to be touched on, it was only because I was still at work on that novel which was the cause of all this trouble. It was impossible sometimes to avoid opening this old wound in order to figure out how to avoid any "similarities". And if anything was ever said, it was done discreetly with one or two friends, while Turgenev, as was made clear to me by so many questions which were addressed to me about him by different people, had been making such a fuss about how I was always putting him down and slandering him. Even total strangers had been sent to pump me about how I felt about him. I, of course, kept my own counsel, saying nothing about either the past or his new stories which had "parallels" with *Malinovka*, such as *Fathers and Children* and *Smoke*, and simply keeping my mouth shut, since the former I had just skimmed, and read none of the latter until last December. Turgenev had sent it to me, and I had begun it twice, and twice gave it up after one or two chapters. I found it vapid, dull – more like journalism than art! All those conversations between the generals and between the nihilists could well be described as "conversations in the kingdom of the dead", the kind that were so popular fifty years ago. So insipid were they! He, who was so good at artistically depicting country life and nature, had no aptitude for rendering life's complexities, individual characters and their idiosyncrasies! His attempts to do any of these things appeared laboured and artificial! In Baden-Baden, I made my views known to Turgenev himself. When he asked me about *Smoke*, I said I found it dull, and that those generals of his never came to life, but resembled waxwork figures. This was the essence of my remarks rather than a word-for-word account. Knowing that I didn't read much Russian fiction, including his, he made a point of sending me *Smoke* to read, so that, seeing the passages he had copied from me, I would not repeat them in my work. All he really wanted was for me to relinquish my novel: in this way he would emerge the undisputed winner. And I would have given up if I had realized in time what was in store for me. But, as I said, I had failed to read his book, and so didn't see what was coming.

Finally, in 1868, in Kissingen and Schwalbach, and later in Paris and Boulogne, I spent the summer completing the last two parts, Four and Five, of *Malinovka*, and, on my return to St Petersburg, put the finishing touches to the whole novel, adding the epilogue, i.e. the final chapters. Having misgivings about the similarities to *A Nest of the Gentry* (something which, no matter how hard I tried, I couldn't avoid entirely without having to sacrifice a great deal, and which now, as it were, had become an inseparable part of the novel), I recounted the entire story of my dealings with Turgenev to Stasyulyevich in order to find out his views about the affair. Of course, he assured me that there were no similarities, that Turgenev's stories had long since been read and were largely forgotten by now. However, when I was reading some chapters of *Malinovka* to him and his wife, she also noticed that "a few things in *A Nest of the Gentry* appear to have been taken from it" – I'm quoting her very words. Never mind that *A Nest of the Gentry* was published before *Malinovka*... Turgenev had foreseen all such comments, and had hatched a plot in order to divert this suspicion from himself and become an obstacle in my path. This troubled me and made me wonder whether I should publish my novel, and even on the very eve of the announcement (in October 1869, I believe) in *Vestnik Evropy* of its pending publication, I told Stasyulyevich that I didn't want to publish it, but I was talked out of it. Turgenev, as I learnt later, was more bothered than I was about the possibility that people might start noticing similarities between his novellas and my novel, even though he and his henchmen would have taken all the necessary steps (and what steps!) to make sure that all the blame would be laid at my door! I have been told that while I was writing the last two parts, he was losing weight and turning yellow, and even then I made a point of locking up my copy books in my suitcase whenever I went out in Kissingen and Schwalbach, never leaving them on my desk, so that he would never have access to those two parts. However, I continued to recount and read those to parts to Stasyulyevich and his wife, and (at that time) I could not conceive of their betraying me, since it would be against Stasyulyevich's own interests, although he was actually in touch with Turgenev and was publishing his minor writings such as the *Memoirs of a Hunter* (and, I believe, 'The Brigadier')* and others. A year before, in the summer, I had read the first three parts in their entirety to Count Apraksin* whom I had met three years in a row when I was taking the waters, and who made strenuous efforts to befriend me. And it was he who, after every reading, made a point of taking notes of what I had read. Also, I read all three parts to Feoktistov and his wife in Boulogne. I had met them previously in Baden-Baden, and it was there that this lady asked me if I could read my novel to her, and whether I would also permit a woman friend of Turgenev to be present. I said I would not, and would prefer to give a reading to them alone in Boulogne. And that is what I did. Count Apraksin, who claimed to be my friend, attended once again and took notes. I didn't have any hesitation in this regard, since I didn't imagine for a moment that someone would part with a treasured possession and just give it away to someone else. Well, that's what actually happened, and people came, took notes and passed them on to Turgenev, who made use of them. It was only later that I came to realize that Count Apraksin and Feoktistov and his wife in particular were stooges, and it was thanks to their connivance that my novel cropped up in the works of Turgenev and others. The same was achieved even more easily, as I mentioned before, in Marienbad, when some people staying in the same corridor as me copied straight from my manuscripts. They were acting under instructions, as I learnt later.

But there is one thing I am not quite clear about, and when pondering the aftermath of all this, I have no alternative but to enter the realm of conjectures. How could well-educated, highly reputed people bring themselves to stoop so low as to commit outright burglary? When it comes to a jealous rival, this is easy to understand. He must fear that the end of my novel, which he does not know, will be worthy of its beginning, and that various extracts will reflect the workings of a single mind and the creations of a single personality, penned by a single hand, thus laying bare the various parts of a big building which have been torn to shreds and ripped apart into a scattering of rubble. Afraid of all this, a jealous rival will try to undermine, pose as well intentioned, whisper my plans in the ears of foreign hacks so that, together, they can get a head start. Well, all this is possible – and that must be what happened! But how a whole community of decent people could take his side in this way is simply beyond my understanding. These are the facts, however! I can only suppose that Turgenev has been slandering and spreading lies about me, as I have always thought, and still do, to the effect that it was never a case of him borrowing from me, but me borrowing from him – and perhaps went so far as to claim that he was the one who was sharing his literary plans with me instead of the other way round. Who really knows him?

There is, however, a contradiction here. For instance, most probably he told the foreign writers Flaubert and Auerbach that something of mine belonged to him (quite some time ago, soon after I had read my novel to him in 1855); but I later discovered that here, when he was talking to Russians, he resorted to a different and even more devious trick, with which he hoodwinked a lot of naive people. That is to say, various people, including Stasyulyevich, gave me to understand that every word of my conversations was being overheard and my every thought followed with close attention, in particular whatever it was that I was planning to write, including my criticisms. Just about everything, in fact. The idea being that I was scattering my pearls of wisdom far and wide along with my imagery, my literary gems, my similes and my metaphors – all just lying around waiting to be picked up and used, having simply slipped through my fingers, since I was nothing but a lazybones, a sluggard – just lying in the hay like a dog, eating nothing myself and giving nothing away to others!

This last comparison was precisely the last point made in the conversation by Stasyulyevich. It was then that I began to notice that Stasyulyevich was acting in the very same way. He said that my manuscripts contained precious items that should be put to use, otherwise they would never become known to the public because of my sheer laziness. This must have been how he had reeled all the fish in! A very smart move! Turgenev's manoeuvre was also well calculated. His hands were freed – without ever being accused of plagiarism – leaving him able to find out everything I would be saying as well as my plan, and always beat me to it, thus allowing him to pose as the great writer, and the alpha and omega of Russian literature, while at the same time blocking my path, and especially preventing me from producing any new or unanticipated work and from catching him fishing in my waters!

He was turning my lakes into puddles and artificial ponds – but there was always a frightening prospect ahead: the exposure of his theft, and that I might succeed in taking my proper place, which he had sprung on like a cat. There had to have been some kind of springboard from which to launch his underhanded whispering campaign of slander and lies. To this very day I do not know what calumnies he invented to feed to Auerbach, Flaubert and no doubt others, which encouraged them (as I shall show later on) either in their own words or by copying my manuscripts, to produce those "parallel" novels (*The Country House on the Rhine*, *Madame Bovary* and *Sentimental Education*). Did he tell them that these were his own work, while accusing me of plagiarism, or just represented them as raw material (whether his own or mine, I do not know) which I wasn't able to complete? To this day, I don't know what prompted them to use this stolen material. Perhaps he was telling them that he had made off with his own material in case others made use of it. Perhaps what all this tells us is that their own creative power was not up to the task, as was the case with Turgenev himself!

I would say "Go to hell" to anyone who came to ask me to write something or other on the basis of their suggestions. I don't mean to say by this that I am a specially gifted writer, but simply that I am self-driven, and that anything that doesn't spring to life spontaneously within me, swallow me whole and consume me – I cannot even think of touching. Turgenev has probably said that he or I cannot cope with this material, and has targeted me with his jealousy. Feeling unable to dig himself out, he has called for help from the west – the German and French. But to rely on this two-pronged strategy – saying one thing here and something different abroad – is dangerous, and if the two approaches were to clash, there would arise a contradiction. Therefore, I concluded at the time, if not Feoktistov and his wife, his stooges, it must have been others who deliberately robbed from me and passed the stolen goods on to others, well aware that it was my property – and, furthermore, Russian property – which they were giving away to become part of foreign literature.

But who? And what for? What possible harm could I have done to anyone, sitting at home peacefully and minding my own business? *That is the question*. A question to which I myself, in the course of these notes, cannot give a satisfactory answer if others, that is to say the culprits themselves, don't shed any light on the matter – on what actually happened. But will they be willing or sincere, and confess to the underhanded way in which they conspired to rob me? Perhaps, if Turgenev slandered me by claiming that I was the one guilty of any dirty tricks, they think, even now, that they were in the right! How strenuously those naive people strove to help him! They took notes and revealed to him everything I was saying, sent him copies of my letters – and not only to him, but to others too, in order to make sure that the dog would have enough hay. What a cunning trick! Customs let nothing get by them, and if I were to write another major novel, they would get their hands on it bit by bit, enabling Turgenev to write another series of pirated stories like *Fathers and Children* and *Smoke*.

Meanwhile, through his homegrown and foreign Bobchinskys and Dobchinskys* (like that historian of Russian Literature, Courrière), he has proclaimed himself the leader of the new realist school of fiction writing, knowing that through this measure he would prevent me from writing and denouncing him. Yes! The leader of a new, hitherto-unknown school of realism! Stealing the work of others before publication, abridging and adding here and there, distilling the essential, altering the setting altogether, dressing characters in new clothes, cutting and pasting, changing backgrounds and presenting it all as his own work – what could be more "real" than such a school?

But there is nothing at all new about this school. When, for example, someone steals an expensive sable fur coat, they never sell it the way it was originally. They cut it up and reassemble the pieces as collars, hats, muffs and so on. However that may be, the fact remains. Turgenev slandered me, and people believed him. When Count Tolstoy heard the first three parts of *Malinovka* at a reading, it moved him and made a tremendous impression on him, and he took a particular liking to me. Only later did it dawn on me, and, as it were, I began to see the light, glimpse the truth, and suspect Turgenev of lying. Incidentally, he strongly urged me to go abroad as soon as possible "and to avoid meeting Turgenev, who was himself travelling abroad". This led me to surmise that Turgenev had been spreading the lie that he had been offering me suggestions and helping me with my writing, or something to that effect. But exactly what, I do not know – no one is telling me anything: they all avoid me, prick up their ears and exchange meaningful looks, whispering among themselves – but not a word to me: they leave me without any opportunity to rebut or refute.

What confirmed my surmise that Turgenev was slandering me was the fact that in the spring of 1868 I received a letter from him inviting me to come and stay with him in Baden-Baden in order to finish my novel. I was left with the uneasy feeling that he was not telling me the truth – that somehow he was volunteering to act as a kind of literary nursemaid for me. Before this I had twice travelled to Baden-Baden from Marienbad, because it was a good place to convalesce among a cheerful group of people. Botkin, Kovalevsky* and Dostoevsky were there among others – and Turgenev too, although he was monopolized by his crowd at the

Viardots', and was not often seen. I repeat, not only didn't I read anything to him, but never talked to him about literature, except once when he read 'The Brigadier' to me, Feoktistov and his wife, and we exchanged a word or two before leaving. Perhaps – well, probably – he took this opportunity too to make up some story about some help or advice he had given me. Later on, I recall, when the novel was being printed, or it may even have been published already, Annenkov happened to remark to me in St Petersburg that Turgenev had lavished praise on my novel, and said that it "had everything"! "But how is it that Turgenev knows everything in such detail?" I asked. Annenkov was somewhat taken aback by this, and suddenly fell silent. Seeing this, I surmised that Turgenev had probably told him that I had been reading from *Malinovka*, or at least telling him about it again, in Baden-Baden – something which, I repeat, never happened.

By this time, I had got Turgenev's number, and had ceased all correspondence with him. This time, it appeared, Annenkov had woken up and tumbled to Turgenev's true character. Later, at least, when I got round to raising the subject, he did not contradict me when I called Turgenev's actions what they were. So Turgenev must have had in his possession either copies of what I had been writing, or verbatim reports of what I had been reading to others!

Once, a common acquaintance of both of us met Turgenev and myself while we were out for a walk in the hills, but did not approach us. When I asked him why, he said to me: "I didn't want to interrupt: you were probably having a literary conversation." Of course, Turgenev let it be widely known that he was either giving me advice or helping me – something along those lines. But in fact he never gave me a single piece of advice or made any suggestion, except for the words "blue night" when I was reading to him the final chapters of *Oblomov*, and had reached the place where Stoltz in Switzerland, after his declaration of love to Olga, called her his fiancée and left.* Turgenev was moved by her "daydream" and her inner monologue ("I am his bride!").* Turgenev felt that I had put in too much unnecessary detail, while she, according to him, was simply dreaming a kind of "blue night", or idyll. "That's an excellent expression – 'blue night'," I said. "Do you mind if I use it?" "Of course," he replied with a grin. And those were the only two words which belonged to him. This must have been the excuse he offered later for using this felicitous expression of mine and claiming it as his own: "Oh, these were all my suggestions and improvements!" How else can it be explained that all these felicitous phrases and similes from *Oblomov* later turned up in Auerbach's *The Country House on the Rhine* and in both of Flaubert's novels, when *Oblomov* had been written fifteen years earlier and published twelve years before *The Country House*? None of this can be simply written off as coincidence. And this is all the more likely because whether I was reading aloud or writing, I was always unsure of myself, and didn't know what to do, and the end result was that I never ever used the words of others except for those two words. While he, so adept at making use of the slightest opportunity, pounced on these doubts of mine, which revealed my lack of self-assurance, in order to spread the lie that it was he who helped me to resolve those doubts. Perhaps, in his generosity, he was even lavishing the fruits of my labours on foreigners, passing them off as his own, thus venting his jealousy, putting a stumbling block in my path, while inflating his own image in their eyes.

Of course, it has often happened that if one of those who have come to listen to me, for example Stasyulyevich or Sofya Aleksandrovna, Nikitenko's eldest daughter (who had been copying my whole novel word for word), happened to notice that something or other was too long or unnatural, then I might cut something, add or change something, but as for the idea that I might add something at someone else's suggestion – never! When it came to advice or comment, no one was as unforthcoming as Turgenev, and it was only on the rarest of occasions that he would vouchsafe a comment: his habit was to listen and remain silent. Still now, whenever he hears a rumour that I might be writing a new novel, he rushes back home from wherever he may be and makes sure always to be seen in my company, so that he is on safe ground when again and again he assures people both here and abroad that I only write when I have the benefit of his advice – or, if you please, his help. If only people knew! Otherwise, if I were to write something without being seen with him, then inevitably the truth would out – and the past would be revealed as a total lie, and he would go crazy!

I didn't fall for that trick though, and two or three years ago I stopped inviting him. Then, a year later, when I was in Boulogne, Stasyulyevich sent me his Paris address, and asked me, as if it were his own idea, to pay him a visit. I didn't ask for his address or pay him a visit. All this slimy manoeuvring and feline cunning were labels that he was – and still is – trying to pin on me. The guilty party is blaming the innocent party for his own dirty work – and, as I can now see, he is trying to besmirch me with a reputation for outrageously cunning, sly and vile behaviour – and putting it about that I am the one begging for *his* company. And this is still going on! Last spring – the same story. One of his hangers-on , in the unsavoury person of Makarov,* came up to me in the *Hotel de France*, where I was having dinner. He told me that Turgenev had arrived and would very much like to join me at my table for dinner and a chat, and had asked him to tell me that. "Do forgive me, a total stranger, for taking this liberty." I replied coldly that I believed I had seen him at Tyutchev's place, and as for Turgenev, "very well, I will see him". But then I added, "Tell Turgenev not to bother about me, because he is only here for a short time. He is busy and I am leaving for Finland." Two days later I bumped into Turgenev on the Nevsky Prospekt. He must have already received my reply. He made a face, indicating that he was not pleased to see me. There was no way of avoiding each other: we had no choice.

"I have a few words to say to you, Ivan Sergeyevich," I began.

He interrupted me to say: "I have no time right now, my dear fellow."

"I won't keep you long," I continued. "I just wanted to tell you that you instructed Makarov to propose that I meet you."

"Never, never! I never said anything of the kind! Who is this Makarov? What Makarov? I don't know any such person."

"He's a relative of Tyutchev, isn't he? And he came to see me on your behalf."

"He was lying – he was lying!" he whined. "I didn't tell him to do anything. He's a rascal. His own family won't have anything to do with him."

And he let loose a barrage of insults and abuse against this Makarov, like the proverbial "poor old Makar" who was pelted with pine cones. This barrage of insults and lies could not have been more vigorous! Later, Nekrasov explained to me that this Makarov was what he described as one of Turgenev's lackeys, or a hanger-on, and that Turgenev had sent him to torment me and to see whether I would receive him. I realized that he had picked this shady character since he wouldn't hesitate to lie if it suited his purpose, by claiming for example that it wasn't Turgenev who had asked to see me, but that it was I who had asked to see Turgenev, or by simply denying that he had said anything at all. He would never have issued such instructions to his other cronies and henchmen, Annenkov and Tyutchev, because they regard him as little less than a saint, and in any case they would have been incapable of such an outrageous lie.

If he had had his way and I had agreed to see him, Turgenev would have known whether I was writing something new – and if I had been, even if I had told him nothing about the content, he would nevertheless, to judge by his previous behaviour, have told both his Russian and foreign supporters that he had in some way or other taken a hand in my work, because, left to myself, I would have been helpless. Either that, or he would claim that he had confided to me something he was intending to write, and I had grabbed it for myself! And if he had got wind of the content, he would have immediately sat down to pre-empt me by writing two or three pages, and then gone around saying that I had been "borrowing" from him, and paraphrasing the material and feeding *his* work to French and German writers, and filching the best passages and passing them off as his own.

* * *

Later, that is to say, last summer – the third I had spent in St Petersburg (1873, 1874 and 1875) – he had obviously given secret instructions to another crony like Makarov, a certain Malein, to find me in the Summer Garden,* where I dined every day. He was, I believe, the son of the archpriest of the Vladimir church, who had served in the Foreign Ministry, where he reached the rank of Senior State Councillor and was awarded his "star" before his retirement. He likes to think of himself as personable and a man of the world. Limited perhaps, well-meaning, but a rough-hewn fellow. I remember, when he was younger, he successfully imitated tragic roles played by Karatygin.* This was one of his accomplishments; another was the fact that when he was in Rome Gogol lived near him and read him one of his own stories. On the strength of this he felt entitled to rub shoulders with men of letters, and I saw him in Baden-Baden – along with Botkin, Turgenev and others – and it was him that Turgenev, having sized him up, thought of as a valuable asset, thanks to his limitations and self-esteem, as a hanger-on and a stooge. It was he who was often seen walking in the park with Makarov, both expecting that I would strike up a conversation with them – of course they would immediately report to their boss whatever I would say to them, inevitably telling him lies about what they claimed to have heard me say about him. But knowing full well what they were up to, I didn't utter a word to them. Finally, Malein came up to me himself, and without my having asked him anything, volunteered to tell me that he had met Turgenev abroad somewhere, and told me what he was doing! It would be wrong of me to tell you that this Malein told me nothing but lies: I didn't know if he would be capable of that. Maybe he was just trying to provoke me into volunteering to say something about Turgenev. He was also trying to worm out of me whether I was writing anything, acting as he was on instructions from Turgenev, and in this he was very persistent.

At that time I had already started work on Parts Four and Five of *Malinovka Heights*, and was not seeing Turgenev (as was well known by his henchmen: it was for this reason that Count Tolstoy escorted me from St Petersburg before Turgenev's arrival there) thus making it impossible for him to claim that he had any hand in it. Therefore, with regard to the parts I have mentioned, he devised another scheme. He told his henchmen, when they left, to spread the rumour that these parts were worse than what I had written previously, and, to prove it, adduced the weakest examples of my writing, and even attempted to convince *me* of that when we happened to meet in the street. Now, these henchmen, who had no expertise at all in these matters, and who believed him to be some kind of a genius, took his words to be gospel. When they taunted me with this kind of talk, I told them that they were quite wrong, and that, except in a few places, the two parts in question were better, more mature, more solid and more profound than the rest. (This is something I say in my manuscript 'To My Critics'.) If I wrote something else to make him stop acting as my nanny, he would still have it in for me. "No good," he would say. "No more of the same old thing! There you are – you see what happens without my help!" Before the publication of *Malinovka*, and soon after it, his anxiety became more and more apparent – especially before! Praise and appreciation of my talent wafted over me from all quarters of society like a warm south wind. In order to divert the slightest suspicion of jealousy on his part, and unaware of the fact that I would be writing the remaining parts, he would make a point of paying me compliments – compliments which indirectly reached my ears. But I didn't let my guard down, knowing as I did that he was weaving his spider's web. He was doing his best to find out what was in Parts Four and Five of *Malinovka*, with which his allies had not succeeded in acquainting him, since I had been reading them only to Stasyulyevich and his wife. And I was trying to find out what else he was writing in order to learn whether he had somehow managed to catch on.

Now, sometime around the end of 1868 or January 1869, I'm not entirely sure, he sent (for Katkov at *Russkiy Vestnik*)* a story entitled 'An Unhappy Woman' (in fact it could well be entitled 'An Unhappy Story'!) But before he left for Moscow, he had instructed his henchmen (either Tyutchev or Annenkov, I'm not sure which one) to stage a reading here for a few people, and to invite Stasyulyevich to listen. You want to know why? I'll tell you. He had learnt that one of the characters in my novel was a rather colourless figure – the gentle, affectionate, long-suffering Natasha. In order to keep up with me and create the impression that it was not him following in my footsteps, but me following in his, he lost no time in hurriedly unloading a story with a replica of my own Natasha. All this to let me know that I had nothing that he hadn't got. Furthermore, he was, of course (typical of him), thinking to himself that I might find out what was in his story from Stasyulyevich, who he knew had been at my reading, and use it for myself, in spite of the fact that *Malinovka* had already been written... The damage had already been done! It was then that I invited him. My manuscript was already in Stasyulyevich's hands – and (if this reading took place in January or February 1869) was perhaps already in print. Stasyulyevich was reading my novel, and knew how much trouble I had been caused by Turgenev's machinations, so the latter came to see me and tried to placate me by telling me that what he had written had nothing in common with my own novel. He failed to recognize, in spite of all the different characters and details piled on by him, that the element of the unhappy woman was the same in terms of her fate and character as that of Natasha in *Malinovka*. Turgenev's only recourse was to claim that all of this was the product of his own imagination, and that I was simply following in his footsteps. As a result, Turgenev ordered his henchmen to see to it that his story was printed as soon as possible, and no later than March, in order to prevent people saying afterwards that he had "borrowed" it from me, since my Natasha was in Part One and had appeared in the January issue of *Vestnik Evropy*.

But it didn't work out that way, and that 'Unhappy Woman' was printed, I believe, in April. Turgenev himself was late in writing her in – since the character of my Natasha was still a pallid one and lacked the finishing touches, so that I usually left her out in my readings – and concentrated mostly on Part Two, with Raisky's arrival in the village. He didn't learn of that until later, and consequently was late in writing his "parallel" story. How detailed and meticulous were his calculations! And no one but myself, the victim, had the slightest idea of what was going on! In pursuit of this goal, the scheme had been set in motion as far back as September 1868, and continued into 1869 with the publication of the translation of Auerbach's novel, *The Country House on the Rhine*, timed to coincide with the publication of *Malinovka Heights*. I didn't pay it the slightest attention – nor did almost everyone else. *Malinovka* attracted enormous interest, regardless of the fact that it was issued in instalments. Stasyulyevich told me: "Early in the morning on the first of the month, crowds of people sent by eager subscribers, who would normally have been descending on the bakery, gathered to buy copies of *Vestnik Evropy*." My novel, with one part in each issue, was printed continuously from January to May. Stasyulyevich reported to me gratefully that the number of subscribers had risen from 3,500 to 6,000. I only heard from Stasyulyevich, who at that time was on very friendly terms with me, and was naturally on my side, that *The Country House on the Rhine* had been warmly recommended to him by Turgenev, who had introduced him to Auerbach, and that Turgenev had arranged everything – that is to say, that the author should have his novel translated from the manuscript, and also published in Russian at the same time as it was being printed in German. In the end Turgenev added a foreword depicting the author, God knows why, as being very akin to our writers, and praising the novel to the skies, as if it were a paragon! He described himself as a friend of the author, and, I recall, even earlier, a year or two before the publication of *Malinovka*, once mentioned to me that while on his way to Paris, he had to make a stopover for a few days in Berlin in order to meet Auerbach. (I heard later that he also stayed with Flaubert for a time on his estate.) I have now come to understand the reason why he felt it necessary to go and meet those gentlemen! I too unwittingly contributed to the translation of that novel. Knowing that the book was extremely long, I recommended Nikitenko's eldest daughter as the translator, as she was well versed in languages and a talented writer. She had already translated many works, including for *Otechestvenniye Zapiski* when they were being published, after Dudyshkin, only by Krayevsky, before Nekrasov. She was extremely hardworking, and not at all put off by this kind of translation from a text in tiny German handwriting.

Stasyulyevich was offering a good fee for the translation: 25 roubles per printer's sheet. I had no idea of what kind of novel it was, and when I asked Sofya Aleksandrovna whether it was any good, her reply was along the lines of "rather boring"! For quite a long time, I believe, I read nothing of his that had been printed. What I heard from Nikitenko and others was just: "Long and boring!" The sensation caused by *Malinovka* silenced him. Rumours reached my ears (and, of course, Turgenev's) that someone who had read *Malinovka* was reminded of the long-standing rift between the two of us over *A Nest of the Gentry*. Also, some gossip was going around to the effect that I had been right, and that *A Nest* was indeed a miniature version of *Malinovka*. Annenkov had also heard a lot of talk, particularly in the English Club, and came to report it to me frankly, adding: "The bigger the ship, the longer the journey." I couldn't help thinking that this reflected well on him, in that it suggested that he rather regretted the fact that in the course of that controversy he had so readily taken Turgenev's side. To me that was the tenor of his remarks. It was as if he felt he owed it to himself to admit that he had been "duped" by the crafty Turgenev – not that he used that actual word, although it was clearly implied. From time to time, he attempted – feebly, I concede – to justify Turgenev's actions in my eyes.

"You were too lazy," he told me once, "so someone else had to take over from you."

"But this *'plagiarism'* is what we call 'theft' in Russian," I said.

"OK, theft, if you like," he repeated nonchalantly in an undertone, and nothing more was said.

Turgenev was aware of the impression made by *Malinovka*, and suddenly, for no apparent reason, published an article in *Vestnik Evropy* entitled 'Memories of Belinsky'. In it he mentioned Belinsky's friendship with him, while at the same time referred somewhat scathingly to Belinsky himself. He also offered something of a survey of present-day literary figures.

"You see," he wrote, "Belinsky would offer his opinion about this or that writer" – and went on to talk about Leo Tolstoy, Ostrovsky, Pisemsky, myself and Reshetnikov,* referring to each with appropriate compliments. His only reference to me was to put me alongside Lermontov. And all this was designed to nip in the bud any suspicion of jealousy on his part arising from any similarity between *A Nest of the Gentry* or any of his other stories and *Malinovka*. Of course, it might be said that because of the admiration he has expressed for other writers, how could there be any question of jealousy? An excellent point! I, for my part, decided to give up writing: so tormented and persecuted did I feel by being spied on and having to contend with suspicion and nervous tension that I folded my arms and announced that I would write nothing more, and out of sheer boredom started reading anything that came to hand, including *The Country House on the Rhine*.

I got a shock: it was nothing more or less than a rehash of *Malinovka* replanted on German soil and with a typical German background. It was full of "parallels", with of course various insertions and additions – but the whole setting, many of the characters, the scenes themselves, the topics of conversation, every single thing from beginning to end was clearly just copied from my manuscripts! It was then that I remembered the obstacles that were placed in my path, which *inter alia* dragged me into an absurd correspondence and robbed me of my peace of mind and the tranquillity I needed to do my own writing. It all reminded me of my experience in Marienbad, where a gang of suspicious characters had been planted in the same corridor. Also, the advice from Count Tolstoy that I should avoid all contact with Turgenev, and his eagerness to see Auerbach in connection with the reading of my novel, not to mention my being urged by certain parties to give them a reading as soon as possible, even before the publication of *Malinovka* (in order, as far as possible, to remedy the harm done to me at the instigation of a deceitful and jealous rival). It had become clear to me that I had become the target of what appeared to be a gang of conspirators... but who were they? And why all this? It ruined my health and made my life a misery! I was in despair and in the grip of a nervous breakdown and fainting fits! It was not only Turgenev that I was up against, but a whole gang of unseen enemies. At every step I was dogged by troubles of every kind and became the butt of malicious sniggering – in short, a laughing stock. It was a virtual state of siege, a mental prison! But who were they? And why all this? It's a question I've long been asking myself and others! I could say, with King David, "My lovers and my friends stand aloof from my sore; and my kinsmen stand afar off."* And they have been doing this little by little and systematically. Whenever I have drawn close to someone and seen him frequently, I have gradually come to notice that my relationship with that person has changed in a strange way. People are paying closer attention to what I say, and taking note of what I do, as well as asking relevant questions, and my responses have then been promptly acted upon in one way or another. I don't usually take any notice of what is going on around me, if it doesn't affect me, but if I do find myself paying attention, then, depending on how much it interests me, I am almost able to read other people's intentions. I may, for example, see that someone is following me in the street – and recognize who it is, whoever it might be, although he acts as if he has no interest in me. But all I have to do is to turn round, and I can immediately identify that person. He is almost always aware that he has been spotted, and in his embarrassment quickens his pace or pretends to be looking in shop windows. When I get into a conversation, I have always been able to detect the purpose of it from its content, even to the point of discerning the significance of every question and every single word. Sometimes I have seen these people immediately after such a conversation rushing home to make a note of it – and it has even happened that I have followed them while keeping out of sight and caught them red-handed. Some of them, of course, have enjoyed doing what they were doing out of sheer idleness and in order to do someone a favour. Close acquaintances of mine – so-called friends – have explained their actions on the grounds that my conversation is so interesting that they don't let a word of it go to waste, and that is why they want to record it. So they have been collecting it and passing it on together with my letters not only to Turgenev, but also to other people who in their turn have exploited it for use in their semi-literary works – and they don't just make use of my words, but also of my actions: you wouldn't believe how many titbits, stories, and even a little comedy, have been mined from this garbage! Of course, it's all worthless. For example, 'The Lover of Phrases' (I'm not sure that this is the correct title of this apology for a story by Turgenev) and later 'A Strange Story', 'Knock, Knock, knock' and so on – all that kind of thing – or copies from my letters, or even cartoon-like caricatures of me.

Of course, for Turgenev and all those who aided and abetted in this plot against me, the goal was to prevent me writing for publication by intercepting my material (they and others thought that I would write this or about this, quoting conversations and letters). Once again the aim was to find out as much as possible about me. Am I really the person I appear to be in letters and conversations, or am I just being a writer and creating or making things up – and if so, what am I like in real life, Oblomov or Raisky... am I a conservative or a liberal? Because all I am doing is telling it like it is wherever I have seen it, even in the most liberal milieux. I have no time for lies in any circumstances, and therefore

I attack liberals when they lie or talk nonsense, and the same goes for conservatives. So who am I? I've been protesting as loudly as I could that I am an artist. What confused them most of all was the inconsistency and fluctuations of my nervous temperament, indeed the very waywardness of my nature (sometimes incomprehensible even to myself), the liveliness of my imagination, accompanied by conflicting impulses, impressions and caprices, whims and so on – in short, everything that is going on in my highly strung nervous system and is part of my delicate and impressionable nature. And my unseen tormentors thought they could make sense of and find their way through this tangle of imagination and nerves in order to penetrate the innermost reaches of my vital, deep-rooted feelings, thoughts and convictions! For this purpose they often recruited any old riff-raff, scoundrels, maybe soldiers, a gang of ruffians who only offended me by their thuggish behaviour, malevolence and effrontery. What lies were dreamt up by those who attempted to police my behaviour and censor my speech! Some tried to blacken my reputation, while others simply failed to understand my nature. There were some, of course, who lied out of sheer malevolence and befouled my reputation at every opportunity.

I have been the victim of this torment for years, and there's no end in sight! The tormentors seem to forget that to subject a human being to this kind of ordeal is an abomination just as bad as robbery – depriving him of his rights, infringing his freedom, his property, his health and his peace of mind! To attempt, by spying and other dirty tricks and police tactics, to penetrate the very soul of a passionate, sensitive and vulnerable body – and not very successfully at that – is nothing but a particularly subtle psychological and philosophical exercise! In the light of these vicious attacks from every quarter, he began to take evasive action, and tried to wriggle out, provoking further outcry: "Aha! There you are, squirming and dodging, proof that you are trying to get away with it! *C'est impayable!*"* Even with close acquaintances of mine, whom they wanted to turn against me, they resorted to Jesuitical tactics. For example, when they learnt that I had said something critical of someone, they immediately let him know, and – hey, presto! – what was once a friend is now an enemy, ready to harm me in any way they tell him to! You see, this whole campaign against me was designed, among other purposes, to purge me of my faults – which, of course, are numerous, in particular imaginary slanders, since (because of my sensitivity, and in no way out of spite) I had redirected the sting of the deadly analysis of which I was the victim to all and sundry, friend and foe alike!

There was an elementary feeling of justice and humanity which had not been included in the equation, namely that it was wrong to treat any individual in such a way, that is to say, to keep his every single movement under the surveillance of a hundred eyes, as if you were counting every single hair on his head – and not just his words and deeds, but monitoring his very thoughts in order to proclaim them to the jury at a mass trial! This is not correcting someone's conduct, but killing someone, and killing him slowly and a thousand times over. If it must be done, then it should be done to everyone, not just one person. And all this because there is something original, some special talent in his make-up. But this is no reason to torture a living person! This is just a total lack of respect for normal, God-given human rights. And what for? To what end? If a man has a gift, surely this is a reason to spare him, and permit him to make use of it – to do whatever he is able and sees fit to do. I have always done my best to spread this message. But to whom? What is the prevailing morality of our time? Absolutely no allowance has been made for something else, namely that I have not had the time to devote myself exclusively to literature. I have therefore had to work and live in St Petersburg, for lack of means, in a climate inauspicious for the pen, a climate which did not enable me to live either in the countryside or abroad like the Tolstoys and the Turgenevs of this world.

I have been mauled, broken like a toy so that people could see what's inside. But in this there were many purposes. Perhaps I will say something about all this if I think it appropriate at the end of these notes. But probably others will do so at greater length (if they should decide to do so). I myself don't know enough about all the ins and outs of this story to write it. All I do know is that this is something that could only happen here in Russia... and that it is stifling me, and I have no way of reconciling myself to it, because I am totally in the dark!

I would like to go back to *Malinovka*. I was really struck by one thing: the similarity between *Malinovka* and *The Country House on the Rhine*. The Volga and the Rhine, the dacha – the big house – and the little house, the one with the grapevine, like the one in *Malinovka*. In my novel there were two German female protagonists, Vera and Marfenka (a pampered young lady), the grandmother, in the person of a professor's wife, a teacher and scholar (Kozlov) and a certain lady – in Auerbach's version with the eyes of Medusa, and in my version with the eyes of a mermaid. At the end, the description of the characters (like Raisky and Vera) and the religiosity of the heroine (like Vera). In a word, all of the first three parts of *Malinovka* have been about that and have been scattered on the endless waters of this dull apology for a novel.

The continuation is not much like that. Here, Turgenev has apparently remembered my initial scheme, which I described to him in 1855, in which Vera left for Siberia with Volokhov – in *The Country House on the Rhine*, Erich and, I believe, the heroine leave for America and the war. Of course, no one (including myself) has the stomach for reading both novels and checking all the words in every sentence for echoes, including word-for-word similarities (in particular, the two or three sentences from *Oblomov* mentioned above, and where the heroine in *The Country House on the Rhine* says, like Olga in *Oblomov*, having decided to marry Erich, "I am his bride", etc., with just two or three words changed). So that if you look at each instance separately, you can assume it's just a coincidence, but if you consider the whole thing, it becomes clear, from the overall plan and idea of the novel right down to the individual characters and scenes, that the similarities are not fortuitous, and there is just one unifying theme with particular prominence given to certain outstanding and exceptional details.

When I told Turgenev about these similarities (when I met him in the street because of Makarov) between *Malinovka* and *The Country House on the Rhine*, he said that it was not his doing – he had nothing to do with it: I should take it up with other people.

"But it was you who wrote the foreword, wasn't it?" I said.

"It wasn't me who wrote it: all I did was sign it – almost without reading it." These were his exact words.

In the course of that brief meeting with Turgenev in the street, I was only able to give him the gist of what I am now writing in detail. He is so confident in his own wiliness, cunning and shoddy manoeuvring that he feels entirely safe in that web of his own weaving – but he was visibly shaken by what I had said. And he is very quick on the uptake! Yes indeed, a veritable mental genius. I would bet that he seriously takes his underhand, lowdown, sneaky deceitfulness for intelligence, oblivious to the fact that any shrewd coquette can lead her husband, two or three lovers and a host of others by the nose and wind them round her little finger on the strength of that kind of intelligence. Ultimately, his wheeling and dealing was favoured by the circumstances, such as his foreign travels and his connections, but most of all by a side plot against me.

At this meeting I explained to Turgenev why I had been avoiding him, and why for a whole year I hadn't invited him to see me or gone to see him either here or in Paris.

"I've seen," I said, "that under your own or other people's names you have been translating my novels into French and German, changing the wording, paraphrasing, picking expressions, similes, scenes and moving them to different places, altering the setting, and so on."

"But where? Show me!"

I mentioned *The Country House on the Rhine*, and he replied using the very same words as before, but, of course, failing to mention who these "other people" were and how they could have supplied Auerbach with every single detail of my original plan, which was unknown to him and anyone else. He had even included those passages – even the ones from *Oblomov* – which he had enjoyed so much during the reading!

"Those similarities could not have occurred by chance!"

"Are you seriously accusing me of producing rabbits out of a hat? I don't have such tricks in my repertoire," he said. "You once described me as a clever cheat!"

I don't remember having said that, but it could have been in the course of the correspondence between us at the time of our quarrel about *A Nest of the Gentry*. I think that instead of "cheat" I used the expression "card sharp".

"Well, I don't know! Very well, let's say it was others who were involved in *The Country House on the Rhine*, but the two French novels?" I pointed out.

"I give you my word of honour!" he broke in heatedly. "And as for the two French novelists, I didn't breathe a word about you." ("So it must have told the Germans," I said to myself. "But what exactly?")

"Oh, I've no doubt that that's true," I said, "but why would you introduce me to them after having given them the whole of my novel, and made two out of it?"

"But why would I have done that?" he asked.

"Out of jealousy," I replied unhesitatingly.

The moment I uttered the word "jealousy", Turgenev could only flinch. He turned as white as flour, and his facial muscles suddenly clenched and shuddered. If anyone else had been present (we were at the Catherine Canal, which we had happened to reach after turning off the Nevsky Prospekt without realizing it while we were deep in conversation), he would have seen that my words had hit home.

"No, no!" he mumbled immediately. "I would have chosen a talent greater than yours, if I were to be jealous of anyone."

I couldn't help admiring him when he said that.

"I wonder who he would have chosen," I said to myself. Those who were writing at that time included Druzhinin, Grigorovich ('Stories of the Countryside'); Dostoevsky had written *Poor People*;

these are all talented writers, but not of his kind. In terms of genre, he and I alone were rivals. But the important thing was that none of the others shared with him their literary ambitions. This was a fact that he was anxious to erase from my memory.

"No, no, neither you nor I are the leading writers," he muttered. ("And what could be the leading writers of our time! That's how schoolboys talk!" I thought, looking at that "number one".)

"So who do you have in mind?" I was curious enough to ask. "Ostrovsky?"

"No, Count Leo Tolstoy."

(But at that time, when these "borrowings" from me were occurring, Count Tolstoy had so far only produced his war stories.)

In a word, he was embarrassed that people were presumptuous enough to guess what he was up to: so convinced was he of the impenetrability of his designs that he himself was at a loss for words.

"That's enough! Ivan Sergeyevich," I said. "You've been doing your level best to be number one, while trying to give the impression that the idea has never entered your head, and that it was beneath you, while all the time you were weaving your web of intrigue." At these words he flinched visibly, and even shuddered. "People have already been telling me that after *Memoirs of a Hunter*, 'First Love' and 'Asya', you have nothing left." And people have really been telling me this – including, by the way, P. O.* "You," I continued, "are working very hard abroad to propagate the idea *que la littérature, c'est moi.** That is to say – you. You take possession of my writings, take them apart and change the settings, while keeping the psychological lining, and pick out the best bits and even individual sentences; you make copies of conversations and whole scenes, and follow step by step in my footsteps in whatever direction they take…"

"Yes, yes!" he interjected with a grin on his face and a shifty look. "Yes, you've described it exactly!"

"I still have in my possession some letters stating precisely when my novels were written," I said.

At this, he responded with a strange and enigmatic smile. I had an idea of what it might mean. When I was telling Stasyulyevich about this, I added that I would have preferred to forget about all this – and I would have, if it hadn't been for *Malinovka*. Since I had already published it, whether I or Turgenev liked it or not, people would be talking about it.

"In any case," I added, "I have already burnt almost all of the relevant correspondence" (Stasyulyevich, who had subsequently drawn closer to Turgenev, had, of course, shared these words with him) "with, however, the exception of two or three letters which had survived and referred to my novels."

"That's all very well," he suddenly remembered, "but after *Malinovka* you didn't write anything. Then where did my writings come from? Did I get them from you?"

(He meant trivial stories published after *Malinovka* such as 'The Brigadier', 'Knock, Knock, Knock' and others.)

"Those were filched from the plots extracted from my letters and passed on to you!"

He was dumbfounded and looked at me with astonishment, having realized what my source was!

"It was a pack of lies!" I continued. "You tried to put the blame on me for what you yourself were doing, and went round craftily creating the impression that it was me 'borrowing' from you instead of the other way round, thus turning the truth upside down!... Nothing but a pack of lies!"

He interrupted me to say, "So now you're trying to suggest that I told Makarov to tell you that I wanted to see you, when I had told him nothing of the kind."

"Another lie! I don't attach any importance to this," I said. "Forget it!" (I was getting fed up with all this. It was all so clear to me. All that underhand manoeuvring by his cronies and hangers-on, the spying, the scare tactics – anything to prevent me writing.) "I won't attempt to apportion blame or responsibility, but one thing is clear: an attempt is being made to create a rift between us, as if someone is relishing the antagonism being promoted.

I don't know what the purpose is. All I do know is that there was no bad blood between us before, and there won't be any afterwards – those 'similarities' could not have come about by chance! Now, this is what I am proposing: we should avoid contact and revert to our relationship before the death of Druzhinin. Perhaps that would make our lives easier. Before, we neither spoke nor met. If we should happen to run into each other, I am prepared to acknowledge you."

"Very well, let's do that! We don't even need to acknowledge each other!" he exclaimed in a bad-tempered manner. "To hell with you! You think I'm jealous? No way!"

And on that note we parted. I've been careful to report the conversation word for word. I have no idea what he told his friends. I have told this only to one or two very discreet persons, and I think that they have kept it to themselves. Let me now take a step back. While *Malinovka* was being printed, in late April the complimentary remarks dried up, although certain comments in my favour did reach my ears via third parties. One person said in an undertone: "For goodness' sake – I mean, I've known *Malinovka* since 1860!" Of course, as I thought, Turgenev had already put in his oar and stealthily added a drop of poison in his attempt to sabotage the success of the novel. And that's what happened! I was keeping my ear close to the ground, but no one said anything to me. However, it so happened that someone started talking to me about *Madame Bovary* by Flaubert, and asked me whether I had read it. I said I hadn't. "But please read it," people told me. "It's delightful!" And they heaped praise upon it. So I got the book, and began to read it, but the picture of the *mœurs de province*"* as described therein (I don't know anything about that from my own experience) I found dull. So I put it aside. And quite some time later, after the publication of *Malinovka*, when I heard the book mentioned in connection with some of the characters in it, I read it carefully, although I must say it wasn't an easy read, since I had to pick out from quite a different background and way of life the details of the behaviour of the two or three principal characters.

I did recognize in them similarities with those in *Malinovka* – in particular the doctor, the heroine's husband, is like the teacher Kozlov; Madame Bovary, his wife, is like Ulinka, Kozlov's wife; and there is also a student (like Raisky) who had known her as a young woman and had fallen in love with her, and later reunited with her, as Raisky did with Ulinka. In other words, the plot of the novel, its plan, its protagonists, the events, the psychology are a replica of the episode of Kozlov and his wife. But all this was so skilfully buried in the mass of detail of a different background and additions that one would have to be as familiar as I was with *Malinovka* in order to recognize the similarities.

"Then, in that case, there simply are no similarities!" people will say. But they are wrong: *there are*! If you were to read both of these books, you would ask yourself what is the difference between the characters of Kozlov and Doctor Bovary – after all they are the same type! But if you were to translate *Malinovka* into French, then our dear patriot, Ivan Sergeyevich, would be quick to tell us: "Oh, no! There's really nothing French about that!" – and that obviously it was not penned by a French hand, nor in a French spirit, but of course by a Russian author who had borrowed from a French writer, something made clear by the fact that *Madame Bovary* was published in 1857 or 1858, according to an article on the subject by Émile Zola* in *Letters from Paris* (*Vestnik Evropy*, September to November 1875), which brought sudden fame to the author and even led to a court case because of the immorality of the heroine! Well, I had blurted out the entire novel to Turgenev in 1855! Every word of it! I now recall that I had made a point of describing Kozlov's career as a student, his lack of savoir-faire, his poverty, his unsociability, how the young Ulinka and his friends made fun of him and how she snatched his cap while he was too busy eating to notice! I gave the same treatment to Doctor Bovary, but did so in order to eliminate any outward similarity: Bovary was married to a second wife and was a glutton, something he had been since childhood. In addition, I created numerous many other episodes and characters. His jealousy prompted him to take my material and keep it for himself. When I was reading my novel to Turgenev, I had dwelt on these details. "So, you see, it couldn't have been the fruit of your imagination: it must have come from someone else!"

When I was recounting my novel to Turgenev, I would dwell on these details and then described Kozlov's character as a teacher, his kind-heartedness, his learning and the unscrupulousness of his wife. Of course, I hadn't recounted in detail the final scenes, because I couldn't possibly have contemplated them at this stage, so the similarities are limited to my first three parts, but in the case of Madame Bovary it was a different matter. Turgenev obviously remembered the type of character (immediately after I had told him anything he would write it down – otherwise he wouldn't have remembered it), and the two of them worked on it, invented an absurd personality and have her commit suicide, something which Zola quite rightly took him to task for in his *Letters from Paris* review. I was almost reduced to tears when I described how much her husband loved Ulinka and forgave her. But they simply drained it of its juice. "*Je ne vous en veux pas,*"* he says so dumbly and feebly to his rival after the death of his wife in the words of Flaubert – and Zola extols this as some terrific, marvellous, *grand, grand, grand* gem of creativity: nowhere else in the whole of French literature is such a profound gem of feeling to be found!

I repeat: what possible excuse can there be for Turgenev to pass on to Flaubert something which he couldn't bring himself to use? How could he have claimed possession? Probably – and here for once I take him at his word – he never once mentioned my name to French writers (see what I have written above). If he had, then I assume they would have wanted to know who I am, and *Oblomov* would have been met with acclaim (as I have previously explained), but he downplayed the whole thing, and I did not care much. Now, however, I can see I was wrong! During that time, he seized the initiative, partly by publishing his own work (*Smoke, Fathers and Children*) and partly by dismantling mine, breaking it into pieces and reassembling it into a different pattern, while systematically preserving the plot, that is to say the content (strictly speaking, my novels don't have a plot as such), keeping the principal characters, shortening and compressing the scenes, and generally draining it of its originality and distinctiveness, thus reducing my book to a limp rag, a mere repetition of what has already been written – and all of this was to be accomplished in another novel with the name of Flaubert attached to it, his *Sentimental Education*. And, as I have said before, he virtually reproduced the first part of *The Same Old Story* in his own *Torrents of Spring*, which he had translated through his agents into every language, like all his other books! Well, why not translate my books, if you feel like it! After all, it's already there in other languages – in the hands of Auerbach and Flaubert, and above all in his hands – and God knows where else!

Indeed once, in relation to these "similarities", when I made a reference to one novel without naming it, he couldn't contain his delight at his own triumph, and wanted to know which one. He gave me a look of triumphant irony, as was only natural, swelling with pride, as he was, in his own genius. For all I know, he has even arranged for a translation of *Oblomov* to appear somewhere or other. As a matter of fact, this book was translated, and not that long ago, into German! *Sentimental Education* was published in 1870. Clearly, a copy was made from *Malinovka Heights* in 1869 (and perhaps his dutiful henchmen had provided him with an advance copy) – but it seems to have been done in a hurry. There was something strange about it: one of his friends came and said a couple of words, and then left. Another one came and had a look – a third rode along the street... five of them had lunch together and talked. One was joined by another, and so it continued!... It was like a moving panorama of the hustle and bustle of a Parisian street scene! It was simply an abridged – and Frenchified – version of *Malinovka*, only it now included bits and pieces of conversation and scenes brazenly lifted from it.

I'll offer some examples, because neither I nor anyone else have the patience to fill in all the details. For example Part One of *Sentimental Education* (1870 edition),* pp. 17, 19, 23, 26, 43,

88–90, 91–167, includes scattered phrases and references carefully selected from scenes and conversations in *Malinovka*. Pages 17–19 contain a passing reference to the character of Fréderic's (Raisky's) mother, the Granny in *Malinovka*: how economically she ran her household without spending money on candles, the visits she received from the archpriest, and also how she would scold her son (grandson in my book), because Raisky turned up late for meals and appointments with her and rushed out to find his friend (end of Chapter 1 of *Sentimental Education*). He "borrowed" a word or phrase from me and put it in his descriptions. He didn't copy the actual wording of the images or character descriptions, because that would make it too obvious to everyone that they were stolen, and it would have caused a major scandal. It was for that reason that the French Courrière in his *History of Russian Literature* (suggested no doubt by Turgenev) classifies me as a practitioner of novelistic painting (*roman-peinture*). But that gives the game away: if the image is as skilfully depicted as they claim, then that makes him a blabbermouth. In art it is only the image which expresses the idea, since it is impossible to tell a story on the basis of words and wit alone (as is the case with Turgenev, according to Courrière). So what you get is not images, but silhouettes, because they are not drawn from nature, but copied from someone else. It is perhaps for this reason that neither *Madame Bovary* nor *Sentimental Education* have earned the major significance in French Literature which was the goal of the combined efforts of Turgenev and Zola, although they did have some considerable success.

Indeed, another reason for this is that the simplicity and naked truth which Turgenev had drained from the Russian novel was not to the taste or liking of the French naturalists' temperament, imagination and outlook on art. Without "effect" it won't work: it's like pepper in one's food, it is necessary to their pampered taste. Every nation has its own frame of mind with its intellectual, moral and aesthetic preferences, and therefore its unique attitudes, so that any attempt to counterfeit it is pretty well doomed to failure, in spite of the considerable talent of Turgenev. He was working to create these parallels even harder than Flaubert himself, who until then – that is to say until *Madame Bovary* – was known only for *Salammbô* with its oriental setting.*

That, anyway, is what I think, but who knows? Perhaps his lies will overcome my truth, for my sins – so it must be – only, certainly not in this particular case!

I would like to make another point: *Madame Bovary*, it is apparent, was something which Turgenev had relayed after memorizing my story, but immediately after it – probably in 1856,* because it came out long ago (in 1857 or 1858 in *Vestnik Evropy*) – and that's why, apart from the reference to the peaked cap of the student Bovary (Raisky) plus the phrase "*je ne vous en veux pas*", expressing Kozlov's willingness to forgive his wife, there were no other literal excerpts from my work like the ones in *Sentimental Education*. Therefore he must have been passing on the information from memory – or from his notes

Later, in *Sentimental Education* (Part One, Chapter 2), on pp. 23 and 26 (1870 edition), the tastes and proclivities of Fréderic and Deslauriers (Raisky and Kozlov) are described quite accurately, as are their activities, except that Kozlov's Latin here becomes Metaphysics (however, his passion for the ancients – Plato – was not forgotten). As to Fréderic, he is arbitrarily credited with a single-minded passion for the novel, as is Raisky (p. 23). He is torn between music and painting (Chapter 2, p. 26), and ends up composing German waltzes (in my version polkas and mazurkas). Further on (Part One, Chapter 3, p. 43), there is a reference to the novel which Raisky had been planning to write in his youth before his major one. Fréderic is also planning to write a novel, *Sylvio*, which is nothing but a close and brazen paraphrase of everything I have said about it. In other words, the novel *Sentimental Education* was taken down in dictation in 1869, when the January, February, March and April issues of *Vestnik Evropy*, containing the five parts of *Malinovka*, were published. The French novel included excerpts from the first three parts. Turgenev didn't "borrow" any more than that, because his aim, as far as I can tell, was to show that he had been helping or coaching me (God knows!), and thus in one way or another that he had had a hand in the first three parts, while the rest was supposedly below par and weak – namely the last two parts, since *everyone knew* that they were written by me when *I was not in contact with him*.

Page 88 (*Sentimental Education*) – the conclusion of Chapter 4 – also depicts Fréderic hesitating between painting and writing a novel, just like Raisky – and this was lifted almost wholesale from *Malinovka*. In boldly taking possession of the reality of Raisky, Turgenev was of course calculating that no one would entertain the notion that the great Flaubert, the author of *Madame Bovary*, would "borrow" anything from a Russian author – including Kozlov's wife, the Grandmother and Raisky: all this belongs to him (Turgenev) and Auerbach, and subsequently to Flaubert, because, supposedly, in September 1868, *The Country House on the Rhine* was first printed in *Vestnik Evropy*, while *Malinovka* first began to be serialized only in January 1869, and therefore I was following in the footsteps of these three geniuses rather than the other way round – while *Bovary* had been printed as far back as 1857 or 1858! And here he was even slandering me! Whereas I was the one who was sharing with him my literary intentions! But how to prove the opposite? Just two or three notes plus those old confrontations. It was all being forgotten – witnesses had died, sometimes my own supporters, and now there is nobody left who remembers! And so on and so forth. That was precisely what Turgenev was counting on – and he has been right so far, and I don't know what the future holds!

On pp. 90 and 91 of *Sentimental Education* the conversation between the artists parallels that between Raisky and Kirilov the artist at the very beginning of *Malinovka*, and on p. 167 of Chapter 6 of the same part, where Fréderic is taking a walk with the little girl, where they are having a conversation and he shows her some books and she tells him how frightened she is of terrifying books – this is a replica of the conversation between Raisky and Marfenka when he arrives in the village but he hasn't yet seen Vera! And he, Fréderic, is doing some drawing for her and reading *Macbeth* to her, and she is scared stiff by the ending. This is then followed by the character of another little girl, a wild one. Everything is mixed up and scattered all over the place, but every so often it is reminiscent of *Malinovka*. The place in my version which is compressed within the identical scene between Fréderic and the little girl is reflected in the single phrase *"Ah, je suis tranche canaille!"*,* similar to that phrase in *Bovary*, *"Je ne vous en veux pas"*. And what Courrière and others have described as the version closest of all to Chapter 3, Part Two of *Malinovka* is the conversation between Raisky and Marfenka when they were out on a walk.

Chapter 5, Part Two of *Sentimental Education* is actually my Chapter 3 compressed into five pages (9–15). Here, once again "borrowed" wholesale, is the description of the neglected garden of an old house and its kitchen garden – but shorter, because only the better parts were included. This is followed by the conversation where Raisky is attempting to seduce Marfenka, but repeated with minor changes, of course. For example, other books were mentioned which were not mentioned in my version. Instead of Marfenka's little birds, we get Louise's little fish – but as far as flowers and the rest of the background are concerned, no changes have been made. In the Flaubert, Louise is just as timid in the presence of Fréderic as Marfenka is in the presence of Raisky, and as intimidated by his education and his worldly wisdom; her conversation is just as childish and naive, and she responds just as bashfully to the endearments of Fréderic as Marfenka does to those of Raisky, while looking out at the river in the distance or watching a cloud go by. Later she comes into her own and changes the subject entirely, talking about French manners and morals, the revolution and the gossip of liberals; and then at some point, I can never quite tell when, the conversation comes to an end: *"je suis tranche canaille"*! – just as when Raisky berates himself for embarrassing Marfenka. But enough of these bits and pieces! Even without them, anyone who compares both novels will immediately see the similarity of ideas, of the structure, and without them will even notice details.

"But if," some may say, "Turgenev encouraged someone, or was encouraged by others, to hand over the content of the novel to Auerbach for his *Country House on the Rhine*, that would mean that all this was happening in full view of many witnesses – and if so, how could Turgenev, and why would he, hand it over to the French? I mean, someone or other would sooner or later figure out what was going on, and the outcome would not be good. Not good at all!" But if it were not the general public which discovered the truth, but rather others such as his accomplices, they would hardly reveal that they had been the ones who had got hold of my material by eavesdropping and taking notes, and stealthily copying my notebooks. But who is going to take the trouble to investigate in detail such similarities between the two novels? Turgenev is counting on the normal tendency of people to say to themselves "so what?" when they discover a similarity or parallel. Obviously, it would never occur to anyone that a French author might make use of material pirated from a Russian author by Turgenev. This was why Turgenev tried so hard to inflate Flaubert's reputation here in Russia and in France.

Turgenev claims that he never said anything about me to the French (and that is quite likely), but what he probably did was simply to pass off my material as his own, having been vigilant enough to check that no one there had translated my work. When suddenly the newspaper *Le Nord** (he was unlikely to have had supporters in Belgium) thought of translating my works in 1869 and asked me if I would agree (I declined), Turgenev was apparently alarmed and, I have been told, left Paris in a hurry. But when he learnt that I had turned down the opportunity to be translated, his confidence was restored and, predictably, he hurried, together with Flaubert, to finish working on the "parallel" to *Malinovka*, *Sentimental Education*. I, of course, knew nothing of this, and did not insist on a translation. And now, it was only the other day that I learnt something else about this conspiracy of theirs: namely, I read in some article that *Sentimental Education* had long ago become known in the Russian press, and had even been translated in the January and February 1870 editions of *Vestnik Evropy* under the title "French Society. *Sentimental Education*, a novel by Flaubert". I have these articles in front of me right now. At one time I had not yet read this novel either in the original or in translation – or, should I say, extracts, because the newspaper had not translated all of it. And if there's one thing I can't stand, it's extracts. As a matter of fact, as the years went by, I found myself reading less and less – especially novels. And now that I have read the novel in the original, I looked through it, and was about to put it aside when my eye happened to fall on the last page of Part Two of the article ("French Society") in the February edition – and I suddenly spotted the name of "Raisky"!

There is a reference to the similarity between Fréderic and Raisky, and the article goes on to say that "Flaubert had a more objective view of his protagonist than I had". Well, of course, Flaubert and Turgenev have shown me the error of my ways and recommended a French approach. Right here in the foreword to the translation of the novel (in the January issue), at the very beginning, it is stated that Turgenev somewhere points out that *Bovary* is the most remarkable work of the latest French school. This was how, with feline cunning, he revealed his true intentions!

One more trick: in the same January issue of *Vestnik Evropy*, in the correspondence from Paris, there is another mention of *Sentimental Education* (pp. 452 and 453), lauding it as a great work! There is even a footnote by the elderly George Sand* hanging yet another garland around Flaubert's neck. I would remind you that there were at that time our own home-grown reviewers of that novel, including Laroche,* who had also reviewed *Malinovka* in *Russkiy Vestnik*. This Herman Augustovich Laroche impressed me as a clever, educated and genial fellow, although apparently, like everyone else, he was somewhat prejudiced against me. But my, how they soft-soaped both the Flaubert–Turgenev novels, although neither were to the taste of Russian readers... They read them, praised them and forgot about them, and that was it! The same goes for *The Country House on the Rhine*. No one was left with the slightest recollection of it. I have already explained why: in order to create art you can't simply say what it is – you actually have to *depict* it. Since images cannot be entirely stolen, they have to be counterfeited – but without a proper paintbrush, all you get is pale imitations, and even if there is a spark, it is inauthentic and not retained in the reader's imagination, and there is no hope of passing it off as a "new school".

My *Malinovka* was published before Flaubert's *Sentimental Education*, and here were Turgenev and his cronies attempting to smother *Malinovka* by foisting both Auerbach and Flaubert on us, and they got away with it!

No wonder that Turgenev was able to pass himself off as the great writer by impressing them with his stolen goods and going around telling everyone that it was all his own work, and that he had been instrumental in the process, contributing details, the plan, whole scenes – all in order to undermine his rival... And boasting how he had devoted practically his whole life from 1855 to 1875 to this noble cause – and while he was at it, posing as some kind of genius. In order to sustain this reputation, he was whispering in the ear of the ageing George Sand that, in this case, it really was his own work. Every year, right up to now, she has produced a novel, each one feebler than the one before, and finally tumbling off her pedestal! In the foreword to her novel *Francia** (published separately), she wrote that it had been Turgenev who had given her most of the material for her novel. My God! What absolute rubbish! Russians arriving in Paris in 1814, even Cossacks; also some prince or other – just a mish-mash of coarse clay, totally incoherent – not even a trace of her past keen intelligence, not to mention her elegance, her depth of characterization – nothing! And now, here she is, it so happens, full of praise (and probably put up to it) for Turgenev's *Rudin*, describing it as "*admirable!*" This is Turgenev's modus operandi:

by hook or by crook! "*Nul n'est prophète chez soi.*"* He knows this, and he made up his mind to find fame abroad, fawning on George Sand and distributing what properly belongs to others to various writers, thus acquiring a reputation as a great writer, the leading light of a new school, and once even sending Annenkov a German article about himself – and Annenkov confessed to me that he didn't know what to do with it. "Send it to *Vestnik Evropy*," I told him. And that was done. Another time, he fell out of a droshky in Vienna, and got someone else, of course, to send a telegram to the *St Petersburg Gazette* to say that he'd had a fall and injured himself, but that the "doctors hoped they could save him". Yet in fact he hadn't hurt himself at all. *Farçeur!** Here, however, people just laughed at him: someone came up to me at the Summer Palace and showed me the report in a newspaper, and said "What a loss to Russia!" But Turgenev influences the opinion of others, that is foreigners, via the Russian press, saying "Don't think for a moment that I am not held in high esteem at home in Russia!" Apropos of birthdays and other celebratory occasions, someone (probably Surovin)* wrote in the *St Petersburg Gazette* that perhaps we should celebrate the birthdays of "Turgenev, Goncharov or Nekrasov" – and leave it at that!

No one else even mentioned it, but Turgenev couldn't wait to react with an article in the newspapers, saying that he was grateful but couldn't accept it, and that it was satisfaction enough for him if he could be of use in this way, etc., and concluded by asking the press to report this. And they all did, including the *Journal de St Petersburg*, which meant that everyone in Europe knows that everyone in Russia, that is to say the writer of the article at least, held him in the highest esteem. In any case, as it is, he is riding high, but that is not enough for him. He wants to be up there with Pushkin and Gogol! "A silly old man," as he was once rightly described to me by Saltykov-Shchedrin* in a conversation. Even Annenkov some time ago once called him "a grey-haired school boy"! Even *The Voice*, in one of its articles, rightly pointed out (respectfully, it has to be said) that both here and abroad he is held in high esteem – *abroad even higher than here, in fact*. And that is quite true – for certain reasons that are all set out in detail in these pages...

It only remains for me to add how he got his own back on me for our conversation in the street, that is to say for my taking the liberty of gently raising the curtain on his supposed *inviolability* – on which he so highly prides himself, and from which he looks down on others. He thinks that it makes him invulnerable, and that those around him serve only to achieve his goals. For his henchmen he chooses either second-raters who are incapable of seeing through him (like Tyutchev, Malein and others) or those who share his views and values...

"Very well, have it your own way!" he responded angrily to my proposal, with an edge of menace in his voice. "Best not to meet again!" And he had his revenge. As I have already mentioned, in order to undermine the success of *Malinovka*, he had even earlier managed to sneak *The Country House on the Rhine* into *Vestnik Evropy* (it was Stasyulyevich himself who told me that Turgenev had had a hand in this), so that it would be published at the same time as my novel, which would be upstaged because of the weight and authority of a foreign writer, and above all because of its similarity to *Malinovka*. Then, at about the same time, he began making references to *Madame Bovary* and also eventually *Sentimental Education*, together with his own commentary and the aforementioned critical comments of George Sand, and finally the similarity between Fréderic and Raisky, which he had hinted at in print. But now, furious with me for the fact that he had been found out, he set about it all again with renewed ferocity – last year, in 1875, in the September, October and November issues of *Vestnik Evropy*, through one among his foreign henchmen, Émile Zola, a self-styled friend and student of Flaubert, while keeping mum like a guilty cat about the mess it has just made.

Yet it was from this hornet's nest that, from September on, Zola published a stream of articles in *Vestnik Evropy*, designed firstly to divert attention from their real target, but purporting to be simply about Parisian society ("Letters from Paris"). The very next month, the very same Zola (an undeniably gifted novelist and an acute, if partisan, critic) started from the outset writing in these very "Letters" about the novels of the brothers Goncourt,* who had been forgotten in France. A month later, in the next issue (November, I think), he turned slyly to an apparent critique of all four of Flaubert's novels: *Salammbô*, *The Temptation of St Anthony*,* *Madame Bovary* and *Sentimental Education*. In reality, however, it was an attempt to remind his Russian readers of the last two, once again emphasizing the similarity between them and *Malinovka*, and thus negating the importance of the latter. This is Turgenev's aim, perhaps craftily suggested to Émile Zola in order to mislead the latter about me. "How was it possible," people will say, "for Zola to trust the word of a foreign writer, and to write so well at someone else's bidding?" We should not forget what a reputation Turgenev had won in the eyes of those French writers, if he had succeeded (with outside help) in placing Flaubert on such a lofty pedestal and in creating a school of his own there.

The fact that he made a name for himself as a writer of great range and elegance shows among other things that, as I have already said, he even made George Sand appear to be a discovery of his own! In a word, he had become their colossus – his every word was law.

Furious as he must have been with me, he now decided to denounce me also to the French literary community. But it was what he said that did the damage. It went without saying that he belittled me, my books and my significance, motivated by his envy, his malice and his inexhaustible talent for lying. Zola and Turgenev shared responsibility for the articles which were published. Flaubert was once again enthroned as a genius – but so what! Who cares? But what was remarkable and meaningful for me alone was this: all the details of his praise of Flaubert as an author, his manner of working on his books, and his methods, such as first preparing a plan and setting it down on scraps of paper, including his thoughts, scenes and random phrases, in case he forgot them, and how he would ponder for years until the time came for putting all the pieces together into a coherent whole – every bit of this had been pirated (by Turgenev, of course) from my letters to various different individuals (conveyed to Turgenev), in which I spoke of myself, my activities, how much I relished my isolation, and all that kind of thing, except, of course, the worlds (that is to say my longer novels) that I had created – the sort of thing that no one cares to share with others. All this was stolen and placed like a horse collar on the neck of this Flaubert! "You had better watch out – if you so much as dare to investigate my dirty tricks and furtive moves, I'll rob you blind and give all that I have to others." And that is precisely what happened! He took everything I had and gave it away.

Stasyulyevich helped him, partly deliberately, partly not. He was clever, adroit and personable, he got on well with people, was usually good-humoured and had a ready wit. I always had a good time with him: his wife was lively, quick-witted, with a will of her own, friendly and straightforward. We became good friends, and I believe she liked me, and still does. Stasyulyevich (progressive, of course, that is to say liberal, *libre penseur,** in terms both of religion and in other ways) had the instincts of an honest man, and a man of some principle. And in favourable circumstances he acted honourably and, on the surface at least, in keeping with his principles. Turgenev, however, seemed to have cast a spell on him like some evil spirit.

The most important thing for him – for Turgenev, that is – was to prevent me from writing any new major work such as *Oblomov* or *Malinovka*. God forbid! Otherwise his whole crafty, carefully designed plot would have failed – not only here in the eyes of his cronies, but no doubt also abroad. It was therefore imperative for him to keep me under close supervision, to make sure that nothing was smuggled through his customs system.

No matter what new project I had in mind, he would always beat me to it, then he would leak the news that he was writing something on the same subject, and then announce that it was his idea and that I was merely like a painter producing a copy – having somehow taken possession of his original work.

Now, in one of my letters to Count Tolstoy, I mentioned something about *King Lear* (my understanding of it) – and then, suddenly, Turgenev imagined I'd got it into my head to write a miniature version, and, lo and behold, his *King Lear of the Steppes* appeared, based on an ugly caricature of that great work, without even respecting Shakespeare, and representing these disgusting products of his work as creations of genius. And all this was meant to be a stumbling block for me, thinking as he did that if I mentioned *Lear* I would only come up with a lousy imitation.

So, as I have said, the result was a series of trivial works ('A Strange Story', 'Knock, Knock, Knock', etc.), all of them taken from those letters of mine – including, by the way, the story of 'Punin and Baburin'!

He was clearly once again lying both here and abroad, telling everyone he was the one who was supplying me with the material, instead of the other way round. And here I was writing something new, when everyone knew we were no longer on speaking terms! For this purpose, in order to keep tabs on me, and having learnt that *Malinovka* would be published in *Vestnik Evropy*, he made a point of aligning himself with Stasyulyevich and started campaigning for him. As I have said, he introduced him to Auerbach, and later to Émile Zola, and finally abandoned *Russkiy Vestnik* and started writing for *Vestnik Evropy*, committing himself *corps et âme,** as the saying goes, and they became bosom friends, seeing in each other a kindred spirit, and the same kind of versatility.

I had noticed very soon after *Malinovka* that Stasyulyevich was skilfully trying to get me to say what I was planning to write next. Of course I kept silent, knowing what he was after. I would hasten to add, however, that at that time Stasyulyevich had no idea what Turgenev might have had up his sleeve, and possibly not even what his ultimate objective was, or even be inclined to believe it, like so many others, because Turgenev was able, like the moon, to hide his dark side from the earth: he didn't live in Russia, and people here didn't know him very well. Here Turgenev was using the same box of tricks that he had used so successfully with previous allies, telling them that I had a wealth of potential and an abundance of imagination – but that one had to catch it on the fly in order to make use of it, otherwise it would get wasted, because I was the lazy dog in the manger, eating nothing myself and giving nothing to others. To the French, of course, he told the opposite about *me*, thus keeping everything for himself – which is quite clear from the way he adapted *Malinovka* to suit French tastes. It was Stasyulyevich (see above) who let the cat out of the bag by telling me that – and began to step up his shadowing of me, and keeping his ears open – when I read him the ending I had in mind for *Malinovka*, little thinking that even this was something that might be filched... which of course it was! In this ending (which would become the whole of Part Six), Raisky had returned from abroad – after stopping off in St Petersburg, where he was to meet Sophia Belovodova – and this would be the conclusion of the episode that had begun in Part One. He would then return to the village and find Granny surrounded by Marfenka's children, and the idea was to conclude with an intimate picture of the family and their working life – of Tushin and Vera (now married) – putting the final touches to the description of their characters.

Just before that, I had recounted all this to Feoktistov's wife in Boulogne. This was turned into a story by a certain Remer in *Vestnik Evropy* (it must have been in 1870 or 1871 – I can't remember the heading), in which all this material from Part Six of *Malinovka* had been compressed and somehow squeezed in! I took Stasyulyevich to task for this, but he remained silent and said nothing to me about this Remer. I suspect that this real or assumed name might well have been used by Turgenev himself.

Ever since then I have begun to distance myself from Stasyulyevich – in spite of pressing invitations from both him and his wife – seeing that there was some kind of tacit understanding between him and Turgenev. Stasyulyevich even hid from me the fact that he often saw Turgenev when travelling abroad, saying only that he saw him for a few minutes from time to time, and he referred to him only casually in passing in order to throw me off the scent. But it was too late: my eyes had already been opened.

Later it became farcical – I mean, the way Stasyulyevich was monitoring my conversation. Naturally I didn't say a word, and in any case there was nothing to be said – although I had a whole new novel worked out in my head. But I hadn't yet sketched it out in full. Meanwhile, I had gathered from Stasyulyevich's demeanour that Turgenev, of course, had promised to put everything in *Vestnik Evropy* (perhaps even without being paid for it), provided that he could get hold of all that I had in mind and filch it for that journal. For Stasyulyevich, of course, it was very much to his advantage for the journal to include a contribution from Turgenev every year, and for him to be a permanent collaborator, whereas there was not much to be hoped for from me – and even if I were to prepare something, it would have taken years... and who is willing to wait that long? To be fair to Stasyulyevich, I don't for a moment want to suggest that he was in cahoots with Turgenev and wanted to help him interfere with my work and cover up his lies. However, he did try to obtain information from me, in order to communicate it to him and get a story from him as soon as possible. He also went out of his way to get me to visit him as often as possible, and proposed that I dine with him once a week and stay until late at night – so that Turgenev would know where I was and that Stasyulyevich was not dozing off.

But I began to visit him less and less, and in any case never uttered a word about literature. It seemed that he composed a story of his own (well, at least the basic elements of it) – 'Punin and Baburin' – and sent the outline off to Turgenev in Paris, claiming, of course, that it was *my* work. I deduce this from the fact that I had at first wanted to write a piece about a perfectly ordinary character for an anthology entitled *Sladchina* (for the benefit of the starving Samarians). This character was a lover of poetry, which I casually mentioned to a few people including Stasyulyevich, telling them that there was a character like this in 'Punin and Baburin' and that the rest was the work of Stasyulyevich – and Turgenev immediately set out to forestall me and composed this garbage. When I mentioned this in fun to Stasyulyevich, he had nothing to say against it.

Turgenev published a few things (but not in *Vestnik Evropy*), in particular a three-page story or anecdote from the French Revolution entitled 'What We Sent' in the magazine *Nedelya*,* so that no one would suspect he was part of any conspiracy against me. It was noteworthy that, in that article, he was currying favour with the liberals by making his hero an artisan from the revolution, while in 'Punin and Baburin' he was flirting with the conservatives – at one and the same time! Now, after I had totally given up consorting with Stasyulyevich – at a time, moreover, when both he and Turgenev knew through their cronies I wasn't even thinking of writing anything, and they had stopped making a secret of their alliance – and Stasyulyevich had openly come out as an ally of Turgenev and was working against me (making use, of course, of the confidences I had shared with him), he was not thinking of attacking me publicly, of course. Nevertheless, it's my feeling that Turgenev overdid it and outwitted himself in his attempt to shift the blame onto me.

Of course, the best way for me to expose Turgenev's tissue of lies and the fact that he has been pirating my material would be to write a major new novel. But at my age (sixty-three) that's impossible. I'm stale, and have even lost the will to live, let alone write. I'm weary of the struggle, of being embroiled in intrigue, and trying to disentangle myself from this net in which I've been caught – I'm in a state of nervous breakdown, and am only able to breathe when I feel calm. Turgenev knows this, and it makes him bold! Furthermore, I am investing all my energies in my literary endeavours, in living my life, and in things that are close at hand and familiar to me; I am hard at work, and it is gruelling, and I am suffering in the way others do who are in love with a woman, or who are in the grip of other passions. I never enjoy the luxury of just one character, just one event, or one aspect of something – but I am always having to contend with the complexities of someone else's life and everyone in it. The toll it takes is dreadful, the brain work is draining, and it only takes some additional anxiety for me to begin to write as if I were intoxicated – a month goes by, two months, then three, and every day the moment I sit down to write I find myself being swept away, and in the evening I'm seized by an urge to finish it all! I'm tired, worn out. And afterwards, when I've finished, I need to wait a very long time before I can pick up my pen again. That's why it takes me so long to write.

Turgenev knew this, and that's why he kept such a close watch on me – in case I were to write something without his knowing and expose him. There is one thing I forgot to mention about our conversation in the street. Once, a long time ago, Turgenev wrote some article or other entitled 'Enough'. I've forgotten it, maybe never even read it. All I seem to remember is that its main point was that, for him, it was "enough" to write. When I met him, one thing I can remember saying was: "Now it's my turn to say 'enough'!" I realized that what was "enough" for me to write was simply grist to his mill. He would more than once try to find out whether I actually wasn't writing anything, and in the summer he would furtively get his allies to go to the Summer Garden to check whether I was writing anything. Malein and Makarov would take a stroll there to see whether I would approach them, but I made a point of avoiding them. One day, Malein finally approached me, started talking about Turgenev and then asked me whether I was writing anything. "No, I'm too old and tired," I replied, an answer he was quick to report to his master. And there and then he rebuked me, and – I repeat – launched a vicious attack on me, claiming that out of sheer spite I was spreading rumours about his plagiarism when it was I myself who was guilty of that very thing. That falsehood itself explains why his henchmen, who had never witnessed any dealings between the two of us and knew nothing about our conversations about my novel, had made it their collective business to get hold of my notebooks, eavesdrop on my conversations, take notes and report to him. (Now, apart from this lie, there were other reasons for this campaign against me, and I may have something to say about that later on.) Of course, they must have been spying on me. I had kept silent for a long time, never expressing any envy of Turgenev. After our reconciliation I only spoke well of him (sometimes to Count Tolstoy among others), as I have said before, expressing doubts about the justice of his campaign against me, having guessed the reasons for it – but later, after *Malinovka* had already been published and I had begun to discover that there were also foreign counterfeit or parallel versions of it in existence, I naturally could no longer contain my loathing of such feline cunning and my desire to defend myself. And here he was, labelling my righteous indignation as envy!

When he found out I was planning to produce yet another ending for *Malinovka*, he too immediately took it into his head to pin a tail or little conclusion on his old story from his *Memoirs of a Hunter*, namely 'Chertopkhanov', a kind of absurd version of *Don Quixote*, so that, if I were to pin a tail on *Malinovka*, he could say: "There he goes, following in my footsteps! No matter what idea I come up with, he immediately copies it, just as he has done in the past!" He did, of course, pin on a tail, and in the same place: *Vestnik Evropy*. Incidentally, it's worth mentioning that, in response to a letter from me telling him that my novel *Oblomov* was doing well, he replied from London (in either 1856 or 1857) as follows: "What a habit you have of harnessing yourself to that ramshackle old wagon, Russian Literature!" You see what a dim view he himself took of it, and how strenuously he tried to put me off it!

Together with the Frenchman Courrière he had long ago referred to my work (in *L'Histoire de la littérature russe*) in the following terms: *"Roman pittoresque, immense talent"*.* But he also said that in *Malinovka* I was imitating his *Fathers and Children*, as well as some Natasha or other in *Rudin*, although I had never read *Rudin* – and still haven't – and don't know what's in it!

Now, this is all I have been able to glean and remember about the dirty tricks used by Turgenev in order to become a dominant literary figure, both here and abroad. In our conversation in the street I put it to him directly: "Over there in France, you make yourself out to be the supremo, telling them that '*La littérature russe, c'est moi!*'* – just like Louis XIV!"

I swear everything I'm saying here about what happened between him and me is true. But I am of course unable to offer the same guarantee for my account of Turgenev's clandestine actions behind the scenes. Readers will see the evidence I have adduced for my understanding, for example, of whatever Turgenev has been saying about me to his allies here and to foreign writers, and how he misrepresented the story of his "borrowings" by telling everyone that I had an abundance of raw material for him to draw upon – or rather steal from me – and telling people that it was he who had recounted his novel to me, and not the other way round. I cannot, of course, prove this, but it is my belief that he did both these things, by telling one thing to some and something else to others. But of course I cannot know this for certain, because other people weren't telling me anything, and I was simply deducing from the consequences, when they came to light (e.g. the novels of Auerbach, Flaubert and others). But, I repeat, *what I do know and can swear to in all conscience* is that *everything that happened between Turgenev and myself, and between me and others, is the literal truth.*

"But who knows?" my presumed reader, who happens to come across these words after my death, will ask. "Who knows?" Turgenev will also have said or written a lot in his own defence, perhaps even more convincingly, being cleverer and subtler than me. "How can we tell who is right and who is the guilty party here?" Both sides, of course, will swear that they are right – the one who is right because he *is* in the right, and the liar who is not because *he* will be lying! So where does the truth lie? That is the question.

"Well, with a 'sable fur coat'," you will be saying, dear reader (which is the example I gave above), "thieves do exactly the same – that is, they cut what they have stolen into pieces which will be made into muffs, collars and hats. Or perhaps, having stolen a lot of muffs, hats and collars, they will make a whole fur coat..."

"So where does the truth lie? Who is innocent and who is guilty?"

All I can say in reply is that the issue can only be resolved by *an impartial outsider who has no connection with the case* – a court, that is to say, of the future, when all the arguments and evidence on both sides will have become available, thus making the truth more accessible. I really have no idea what thieves do with fur coats. All I've heard is that they are likely to cut large stolen goods into smaller pieces and maybe even turn small pieces into larger ones – I don't know. But what I do know, from my own experience, is that, as far as literature is concerned, they tear large items into little pieces, or forge "copies" of the original. I'll let you, dear reader, make up your own mind! You decide whatever is simplest, most feasible and convenient: to take one whole big complex thing and cut it into smaller pieces, reducing its proportions, miniaturizing it, even rephrasing a text, thus dividing it up into separate stories; or to make it into one big heap by amalgamating parts of different books, even foreign ones, or by turning smaller figures into larger ones, and even depicting them as Russian, familiar figures. It would take an experienced critic to determine what is native and what is foreign; who is right, who is guilty and who is telling the truth; what is artificial, subtle, artful and false – and where simplicity and truth lie.

"Are we going to sort out the quarrel between two literary Ivan Ivanychs and Ivan Nikiforovichs?* But who wants to do that? What has the next generation got to do with it?" you may well ask.

Please, if you will allow me: even in Gogol's story, it's not a matter of a rifle or a pig, but of the two people themselves, that is to say Ivan Ivanovich and Ivan Nikiforovich – not just two humble tradesmen, but two human beings! And this is the very reason why you are interested in them at all, and anyway, who cares about a couple of obscure provincials or their quarrels? However, you yourself would not scorn such a description of their lives and habits written by a master any more than other similar examples. The characters in 'Old-World Landowners',* for example, and other such insignificant people. But they're human beings too, aren't they? So as far as my relations with Turgenev are concerned, what is instructive or significant is not so much what we've written, but rather the mores of our time and what is taking place in literature behind the scenes, which I would even go so far as to say is vital for the history of literary fiction – all that busy toing and froing in that anthill. Identifying all these trifling details will lead to the truth – and the truth, in whatever form and on whatever scale, always sheds light and promotes the improvement of human affairs! But this, dear reader, is something you already knew without me having to tell you – and, of course, better than me!

This is the primary reason why I took it into my head – *with the greatest reluctance and much against my will* – to set all this down on paper.

"So why *am* I doing this?" the reader may ask. "Is it for my love of the truth? And only that? Aren't I doing it solely in my own self-interest?" No, it is not for the truth alone, although that in itself would have been a good-enough reason for me to take up my pen. There are several reasons – and more important ones. "Aren't I doing it solely in my own self-interest?" So you're thinking I just want to get Turgenev off my back and recover my stolen goods. *Pas si bête!** I know that "whatever falls off the wagon is lost". As for me, I've lost everything! No! Even now, while I am still living, I am hardly bothered about my literary reputation, in spite of my self-esteem – something which manifests itself in a strange way. When I happen to receive a compliment – something intelligent, elegant and pleasant – it just rushes to my head like wine, but the feeling passes and I sober up very quickly, and doubts begin to creep in. I get nervous and apathy ensues – why do I need all this? Why do I need to find myself on a pedestal after I'm dead?

"Perhaps you yourself," people will then say, "have sewn yourself a sable fur coat out of worn-out collars, hats and muffs, and you now want to give it away. Well, could it not be that Turgenev (that 'modest', 'decent', 'unassuming' gentleman) has given away an entire novel so that foreigners would be inspired to write, and so on and so forth?"

"Anything is possible," I say, and it is hard for me to defend myself, not only against Turgenev, but also his allies. Everyone is against me – *et toutes les apparences sont contre moi*!* They got in ahead of me – they wrote, they stopped me writing, and may well continue to do so if I decide to resume – but *the truth remains the truth*, no matter how you distort it! My situation is what you might call tragic; my whole past is against me; I can no longer write in the summer, because of the need to cool off, because I am so tired, and ultimately because I have written *so much, perhaps everything that I was destined to write*: two or three epochs of Russian life, and perhaps even *my own* (see my article 'To My Critics').* What am I to do with myself now? Suffer in silence – which is, of course, called the cross, which I will have to bear!

I can now hear further objections and questions, dear reader, as I stand in the dock before you.

"Very well, so be it. But if you have been so childish and naive as to give away your thoughts, your images and the whole picture along with its frame, then there's nothing left for you to do except to just shut up and accept it. So what if Turgenev has now become the *leader of a school* – you yourself contributed to his success, and you will remain his imitator. Resign yourself: after all, you believe in Christ and worship him; behave like a Christian – forgive and forget!"

"I would never have wished for anything like that," I reply. But neither Turgenev nor the others will allow me to do that. Let him revel in his reputation as a genius, as the leading light of a school, let him be praised to the skies! I will stay silent, retire to the wings, even refrain from publishing my work, and do my best to avoid being mentioned in the press so long as I am left in peace and forget all this. But in spite of everything that has happened, he will try to make it appear that if I write nothing more, I will still be branded an imitator, and since I will have stopped writing, he will declare victory and thanks to the lies he is spreading and his plotting I will go down as a plagiarist, and nothing but a plagiarist. Let him end his campaign and rest on his tarnished laurels, and leave me in peace! And then I too will stay silent, and that will be the end of it! But, as far as I can see, he is still anxious to prove that I am the one who is to blame and not him, while others are demanding that I continue writing!

And what is more, those *others*, his allies, and witnesses, all those who have become entangled in this deception – well, it seems to me that they are demanding or expecting a response or an explanation from me, as if for some reason they are surprised by my silence, and have hinted quite clearly that after I've gone I should have left something in writing by way of explanation. Meanwhile, no one is telling me anything directly about what Turgenev is saying, and the fact that he is vilifying me, and venting all his spleen and disdain for me with his lies. So, as the reader will be well aware, I have been left in the dark concerning the basis of the many enigmatic overtures made to me. Just on the basis of that meeting with Turgenev himself in the street in the spring of 1874 I got the impression that he was doing his best to present himself as the originator and me as the copycat when I pointed out to him that he was following in my footsteps. And I had not heard this from anyone else. And only the other day, as I have just mentioned, I happened to notice in *Vestnik Evropy*, on the last page of a translation of *Sentimental Education*, that others had noticed the similarity between the protagonist of the novel and my Raisky. No one says anything to me, and I don't read much, but there's something they are anxious to hear from me! So that's the second reason why I have been compelled to write this distressing account! Namely, having no other recourse but to repudiate false accusations. It pains me to face the fact that I too am forced to raise my voice. And this I have done. "*Audiatur et altera pars.*"*

Turgenev, of course, will be speaking and writing a great deal in his own cause, so let others be the judges in our case, and it is to be hoped that the result will set an instructive example! In spite of the saying "The dead are beyond blame or shame", I am still unwilling to shoulder the shame and odium of another in the eyes of future generations: I have enough trouble with my own shortcomings. The jury will undoubtedly rule that they are both good men and both right – in their own way! I reject any comparison with him. But if only they would leave me in peace, then I think I would forget about the truth and the judgement of future generations, because if they don't see that I am in the right and insist on branding me as a thief and a liar, as well as a slanderer, my ashes will turn in my grave. It would only go to show that truth never prevails over falsehood.

I know that I'm being punished for taking such a *casual* attitude towards my own talent, for being lazy, for wasting my youth instead of knuckling down to studying and writing (after all, this is the way we were all brought up and taught, and how we grew up and lived, just as I set out to depict in a number of ways, including what has come to be known as "Oblomovism"),* and for many other things – in a word, for frittering away my talent, something which I barely recognized in myself and was reluctant to trust. Somebody else just grabbed it, took it abroad, shared it with others... and founded a whole new school! Just imagine!

"What a nerve!" the jury exclaims. "You think you're another Dickens, a Balzac, maybe even another Flaubert, the great Flaubert!"

" No," I say, "I don't think anything of the sort." I can now see quite clearly what Turgenev has done and what came of it: namely, that if I hadn't recounted the whole of my *Malinovka* in detail to Turgenev, then the world would never have seen *A Nest of the Gentry*, *On the Eve*, *Fathers and Children* and *Smoke*, which have become a part of our literature, not to mention *The Country House on the Rhine* in German or *Madame Bovary* and *Sentimental Education* in French, as well, perhaps, as many other works which I haven't read or heard of. For example, only recently *Vestnik Evropy* published a translation of *Germinie Lacerteux* by the Goncourt brothers.* It's uncannily reminiscent of the debauched Marina in *Malinovka*. But now I am saying nothing about this. The type is one and the same, that is to say, grown from the same seed sown in *Malinovka*. It has grown a lot – but part of it all has been transplanted by Turgenev onto French soil. And he has put Stasyulyevich up to spreading the word that it was something which had already become known to the French – it's the gospel truth!

"Wonderful!" the reader will say. "So much the better! And you (me, that is) did well to blurt out your rough-hewn novel to Turgenev, and he too did well to share it and give a shot in the arm to French literature and belles-lettres!"

"Yes, that's perhaps the case," I'll agree. "I would even have been very pleased and willing to accept my position had everything been brought out into the open with my reputation unsullied and intact, and my merits acknowledged, that is to say, the value of my work and my ability to put my material to the best possible use. But it was pirated by others, and that was what all the fuss was about. Good for them! Well, who cares! As long as I am left with my truth – something they stole from me, and not me from them! But no! Turgenev's strategy is to turn the truth upside down and make me the suspect and himself the innocent party – something which, of course, I cannot permit."

"But after all," people will say, "even Shakespeare, Pushkin and Gogol did just what Turgenev has done, namely 'borrowed' from lesser luminaries or from run-of-the-mill writers (just as Shakespeare, for example, 'borrowed' the plot of *King Lear* from one of his friends). He, followed by Pushkin, 'borrowed' from legends, chronicles and original sources, as did Byron. It was Pushkin, they say, who gave Gogol the idea for *Dead Souls*."

"All that is true," I reply. "However, these great masters produced great works from 'borrowed' material by informing it with their own creative powers, but without, of course, usurping other people's style, images or scenes! And if they did 'borrow', it wasn't because they couldn't have managed by themselves. Ivan Sergeyevich, on the other hand, 'borrowed' my old lady, the Grandmother in *Malinovka*, and used her again in his *Nest of the Gentry* and *Fathers and Children*. And it's not just me saying this, but almost every day someone or other – everyone in fact – is commending my 'old lady', the Grandmother from *Malinovka*, as a portrait from life. But you'll never hear anyone say this about Turgenev's old ladies! As for Raisky, all Turgenev has done is put a bit of him in Panshin and another bit in Lavretsky – both of them pale imitations. 'An artist who created images not out of his imagination, but out of his mind!' – that was what Courrière said. What rubbish! And as for me, do you hear, it's come from my heart! After all, if, as they claim, I'm a painter, and yet at the same time a conveyor of ideas, then I must be an 'artist'! Behind any image worthy of the name there must be a thought which tells us something about the time as well as its mores. And if we add to this the heart, then that completes it. Therefore, when Turgenev transforms something, he doesn't turn it into Shakespeare, Pushkin or Gogol, but rather a typical Turgenev miniature, and he is not so much creating as composing, and trying to turn what are nothing but tiny, barely noticeable mannikins into full-size figures and force the pieces into his plan in order to make up a threadbare story. And whatever he doesn't succeed in integrating into the plot, he puts into the mouths of his characters. Take, for example, the conversation between Potugin and Litvinov in *Smoke*: it's simply a continuation of the conversation between Raisky, Volokhov and Kozlov in *Malinovka*, in the same way that it is later to be partly repeated in *Sentimental Education*."

"Nevertheless, it is he who emerges victorious," you will say. "*Smoke* and *Fathers and Children* were published long before *Malinovka*, and *The Country House on the Rhine* and *Sentimental Education* came out at the same time as *Malinovka* or later!"

"Ah yes, that was such a crafty move! And I was left helpless, although it was still necessary to make my voice heard. But I'll leave it to others to judge. Why? I'll answer that with a question: 'If everything I have written here happened exactly as I have described it, should I have written it or not?'"

So much for this brief account. I shall now turn to an overall summary of this whole business.

I have said that, apart from these two reasons which prompted me to tell this pathetic story – i.e. (1) a natural need to defend myself against this lie and to give a true account of this long-drawn-out and treacherous plot, and (2) the necessity imposed by others on me to voice my rebuttal of the accusations levelled against me – I have even more important reasons. But before I come to them, I need first to reveal how I see things now – to wit, the true reasons for Turgenev's permanent stay abroad. Even before 1855 he had spent a long time in foreign countries. He once told me that his mother gave him only a small allowance, and that he had left for Paris as a young man and, penniless as he was, was taken in by Viardot. He told me the funny story of how, in their absence, he lived in their country house for a whole season and ate up everything that was edible in their garden since he had no money. I got to know Turgenev at the end of 1846, or rather at the beginning of 1847, when he published his version of *The Same Old Story*. I had never met him before then. Later, in 1855, people began to be allowed to travel abroad, and Turgenev, as I have already mentioned, practically settled there, only returning from time to time, either to St Petersburg or to his estate.

The first reason for this absence from Russia was, as he announced publicly, his affection for the Viardot family. This is not the right place to say any more about this particular reason, although it is perfectly correct. I will just say that he was unable to conceal his pride about his friendship with the famous singer. It was a feather in his cap and lent piquancy to his own celebrity! And it was there that he had an illegitimate daughter by a peasant woman, raised her and saw her married – something he bragged about among his circle of friends.

The second reason was his absolute dread of being exposed for what he was. His affected humility and easygoing camaraderie, his velvety, feline manners, all of which masked his malice, his secretiveness, duplicity, egotism, pretentiousness, selfishness and hypocrisy, his dissembling, his dandyism, bordering on fatuousness, combined with his desire to cut a dash with women and

pose as the leading literary luminary – all of this would have
been exposed in two or three years if he had remained here for
any length of time. By now, some people had succeeded in seeing
through him; they had noticed how frequently he lied in trivial
matters, always boasting and showing off in total disregard of the
truth. Dudyshkin was shrewd enough to see through his mask.
Belinsky was apt to tease him at times about these habits, although
not altogether directly. But all this was hidden behind a veneer
of a hail-fellow-well-met manner and a reputation as a gifted
writer, as well as his affability to one and all. He was hospitable,
an amusing and witty conversationalist, and gave dinner parties.
For all this, his true nature had a way of revealing itself, so from
time to time he would scuttle off abroad. Take his relationship
with Nekrasov. The closest of friends to begin with, and then a
rift. Nekrasov would often complain about his subsequent pattern of behaviour, and began to write a memoir revealing some of
his letters and so forth. There was also some trouble with Count
Tolstoy and a falling-out.* Later, Turgenev and I quarrelled once
more, and he saw fit to ally himself with Stasyulyevich, whom I
then began to steer clear of, and I ended up telling Turgenev that
we should stop seeing one another. He rushed off to Moscow to
make his peace with Count Tolstoy and got together with him
again, so I heard, after a long estrangement. All these break-ups
with various parties did not speak well for his own reputation.

In Paris and Karlsbad, Turgenev was at pains to cultivate Count
Alexei Tolstoy, who died last November.* Both Turgenev and
Stasyulyevich followed him around all over the place, and after
his death proclaimed themselves his "friends"! The count was
cordial with everyone, but privately formed an accurate opinion
of both on the basis of Turgenev's attitude to me, as well as that
of the capricious character of Stasyulyevich, which turns this way
and that like a weathercock, depending on where the wind was
blowing. When the drama *The Death of Ivan the Terrible* was produced in Weimar in a German translation, Turgenev made haste
to write to me with evident satisfaction that it was "a flop" and

did not even warrant a *succès d'estime*!* Upon his death, both of them posed as friends of his because they had spent the summer together in Karlsbad and because the count had published his last pieces in Stasyulyevich's journal. The count enjoyed a reputation as a man of honour.

Turgenev, of course, lives abroad discreetly and quietly, giving nothing away. In this way he wears two masks! When he begins to feel uncomfortable here and finds that he is being scrutinized too closely, he leaves for Paris.

The third and most important reason is his literary ambition. This manifested itself in 1855 when I put into his hands my entire literary assets by recounting to him my *Malinovka*. He had dried up. *Memoirs of a Hunter* had begun to pall, and there was pressure on him to produce something major. Thereupon, I repeat, he put this down to a problem with his bladder that he claimed had been caused by the Paris climate, which prevented him from working – and confined himself to minor but charming miniatures, glittering with sparks of poetry, with frequent references to country life, nature in general and simple folk. There were porcelain cups, or snuffboxes decorated with tiny expensive illustrations! Suddenly he came upon a windfall not simply of material but of ready-made characters, entire scenes, together with a particular style of writing! It was above all this, I can now see, that prompted him little by little to move to Paris, selling off his estate piece by piece (as I understood from Annenkov) and taking the proceeds with him, along with the literary property he had stolen from me. Up to that point he had been hiding his literary impotence from us, but now he went off carrying away another person's talent with him and presenting it as his own, with the implication that in Russia there were no people except ignorant country bumpkins on whom such treasures would be wasted, incapable as they were of appreciating them. It was from behind this mask that he hid his thefts and his own imposture from others!

It may be that his idea is to pretend that, back home, he's afraid people may steal from him – who knows! He hasn't yet managed to establish a total monopoly because, as is apparent from his letter to me, I have been repeatedly recounting to him passages from my novel, in the presence of witnesses – Dudyshkin, Druzhinin, Botkin (so that once, in the course of a reading or a recounting of his work by Turgenev to Druzhinin, the latter remarked in one place that it was something he had heard before from Goncharov). And apart from these passages, I might well find myself sharing, or having already shared, passages with others anyway, including Nikitenko and his family – and when I began to write them, various people made copies of them. But he already knew that after *The Same Old Story*, which had been quite a success, I had already completed *Oblomov* – and therefore his *Memoirs of a Hunter* would be unlikely to beat me to it, especially if I were to follow it up with *Malinovka* and he produced nothing in the mean time. So he started dividing up the novel I had been reading to him into separate parts – one of which he kept for himself while disposing of the others here and there. But here in Russia that was impossible to do, that is to say, to distribute them among his cronies – or anyone else. And if it turned out to be garbage, it wouldn't have been to my detriment, while any thought of enhancing my reputation would have been out of the question. It would have stuck out like a sore thumb in our literature – and would have meant his downfall! Indeed, decent people would never have gone along with such an idea: he somehow needed to tarnish my reputation with lies, something that wouldn't have worked here in Russia: I was too well known here, and the lie would immediately have been exposed for what it was.

He left for Paris, where he surrounded himself, in the literary community, with Goncourts and Flauberts and God knows who else, sharing with them the episodes and characters which I had described to him in detail, and which he had not used himself. In this way his stature grew enormously, and he became their guide and mentor, lecturing them on the significance of the naturalist school beginning with Gogol, and passing over the rest in silence, except for himself.

Of course he forbade them even to mention his name – and that is how and why, in 1857 or 1858, *Madame Bovary* came to be published, written with a simplicity of content, style and plot that was totally new to French literature. But it was something totally off the shelf, while other genuinely talented Frenchmen such as Émile Zola, Daudet* and others understood the significance of our naturalist school and independently followed what was for them an entirely new path. Strictly speaking, Turgenev was their teacher – I mean, of the emerging young writers – and it was to this that he owed his importance. Twenty-three years later, in *Sentimental Education*, a character finally appeared (soon after *Malinovka*) who was based entirely on my character of Raisky and in a similar setting. I have never read the Goncourt brothers, so championed by Émile Zola in *Vestnik Evropy*, or Flaubert (just a couple of things recently perhaps, but not very much). But as a result of Zola's critique I began to see (and from the Goncourts too, and possibly others) a marked similarity with the naturalist school, largely in terms of the psychology of the characters, but also of the plot, rather than the external features. Most probably, Turgenev had been horrified by the plot of my novel when I had described it to him, and thought of me as a colossal talent (a view which I, of course, did not share), and he spent half a lifetime trying to credit others with it while building a pedestal for himself on which he could stand.

So much for the principal reasons why he moved abroad. I will now turn to the reason, also very important, why I have felt compelled to write all this. It should be obvious by now (as it is to me, at least) that the reasons why Turgenev absconded were petty, selfish and discreditable. He has a different explanation to offer, of course. He dresses himself up in a lion's skin and poses as someone dissatisfied with Russia, and that as a result he left of his own free will. He once wrote in the press: "When I saw what was happening here (that is, in Russia), I threw myself headlong into the German ocean",* or something of the sort – in other words, the ocean of Western science, freethinking and freedom of action, a world of art, ideas, humane principles, an escape from our own benighted, oppressive and narrow beliefs, sentiments and convictions – so that he could live and act in the name of humanity, etc., etc. In short, following the example of Herzen and Ogarev* and others thirsting for freedom, genuine émigrés, cosmopolitans! It's total garbage, a pack of lies! The reason why he threw himself into the German ocean was not because he couldn't stand Russia any longer: in France he could live without restraint within a circle whose members were unable to see him for what he was, because he was a foreigner and they were thus unable to see his hidden dark side – the very reason why he spent so much of his time out of our sight abroad.

This is what cosmopolitans say or think: "We refuse to recognize the narrow confines of nationality and patriotism; what we recognize is mankind, and we work for its good rather than that of a particular nation. You Russians sit tight with your orthodoxy, your autocracy, your nationalism – and do so under the oppression of these three principles which surround you on all sides like the sea, until you are overwhelmed by people who are enlightened, free and maturely developed, the whole of mankind united, without labels of nationality, religion or regime! 'Look around you,'" they say, "'Japan is already flourishing, China is on the move; from the West, new ideas are on the march along with big guns and colossal capital. England and America are setting everyone the example of independent development and self-government – and spreading it around the world! And here you are, still in your infancy, dependent on your mummies and daddies regardless of the fact that even the biggest brood hen cannot hide all her year-old chicks under her wings! And here you are crouching under these wings with your arms and legs splayed and hiding your head! Meanwhile, the Anglo-Saxon races – the English, the Americans, the Germans, not to mention the lively, mobile spirit and intelligence of the French, are spreading over and transforming the whole world, a free world of free and mighty peoples, and the whole of mankind is overwhelming you! And you still don't dare even to think, raise your voice or even move freely. Your mind, your spirit, your thinking and your will are stifled. You have neither science, nor art, nor even free trade, and therefore no independence. Your much-vaunted national strengths and abilities are going to waste, crushed by servility, indiscipline, fear and pathetic infantilism. And to this very day, it is foreigners who do everything for you: they teach you, they keep you healthy and attend to your material and spiritual needs! You are poor, pitiful and helpless – you are nothing but infants and slaves! We are leaving you and will live with mankind and for mankind!'"

That, in a nutshell, is the cosmopolitan's message. I don't know whether, in this comprehensive dream of the future when the peoples of the world will be gathered into a single family (and there will be no such thing as nationalism or patriotism, but only a universal brotherhood in which everyone loves his neighbour), there will be room for a modicum of justice: that is not for the likes of me, a blinkered patriot, to judge.

However, this is nothing but sheer sophistry!

No one of any nationality can take it upon himself to put this idea into practice, even supposing that there were the remotest prospect of doing so – any more than a soldier, even if he were capable of taking such an ultraphilosophical and unconventional view of warfare, cannot leave his own side and go over to the enemy without disgracing himself. A citizen of any country, no matter who he might be, is nothing but a single unit, a rank-and-file soldier, and cannot by himself answer for and make decisions for a whole developed nation. Even if in theory, philosophical or otherwise, he can draw conclusions or formulate advanced doctrines, he has no choice but to be subject to the circumstances that are current at a given moment. Even if all nations were to coalesce into a single mass of mankind after nations, languages, governments and so forth had been eliminated, it could only happen after each of them had made its own contribution to the kitty of mankind, a contribution consisting of the entire assets of the nation – intellectual, creative and spiritual, including its will.

Each nation is born, lives and commits its resources and efforts to the mass of mankind, lives out its life and disappears, leaving behind its ineradicable traces! The deeper these traces, the greater the extent to which a nation has done its duty to mankind.

Therefore every renegade who has turned his back on his country and who has failed in his duty towards himself, his land and his fellow citizens is a criminal – even from a cosmopolitan's standpoint. He is nothing but a deserter. That is why patriotism is not only a sacred and lofty sentiment and duty, but it is also a practical principle which should be as much second nature as religion, honour and national leadership for each and every member of an organized society. One's first duty is to one's people, and then to mankind as a whole. All lofty, sacred and pure ideals are nothing but the embryo of an idea, and ideas themselves in their turn are forerunners of the rules which constitute the practical principles of life. And what if this utopia of a united humanity were never to come to pass, and generation after generation were to carry on focusing only on their own self-interest and working for themselves as well as for mankind as a whole, and continue to do so until the end of time? In that case, God knows what name you could give to these voluntary exiles...

Everyone knows why Herzen and others like him (who knows how many there were?) acted as they did. Fearing disaster, they ran away from threats in search of greater freedom. Herzen, without losing sight of the cosmopolitan idea, was nevertheless acting in the best interests of Russia. Because of his great love for his country, he detested its shortcomings, was at odds with its government and made demands of one kind or another only for its benefit. He denounced abuses – and was without doubt a great asset to Russia, and opened our eyes to ourselves. He left because here he could not do any of these things.

Ivan Sergeyevich was not threatened by any particular difficulties: everyone found the censorship cramping and oppressive (among many other things); we had no freedom; later things improved. I am not saying that everyone had to stay here in

Russia, come what may, out of sheer jingoistic patriotism. Not at all! After all, why shouldn't you leave, if you have the means and living abroad suits you, and there is no pressing need for you to stay here? I am only venturing to probe into Turgenev's personal reasons (apart from his particular affection for that nation) for virtually settling in France, and then putting on airs as a fastidious gentleman who had found that there was no one worthy of him in his native land! In one sentence: "When I saw what was happening here, I threw myself headlong into the German ocean."

But this was not the half of it. What he omitted was as follows:

"Having accumulated enough literary capital to last a lifetime, and in order to use it to obstruct my compatriot and rival, I must distribute what I have taken with me among German and French writers; I must found and head a school and prevent the works of my rival being translated into French, and become the sole representative abroad of Russian literature and build myself a great reputation both at home and abroad and become the equal of Pushkin and Gogol and destroy Goncharov along with his novels by tearing them to pieces." This was his thinking, his goal and motivation. And this could only be achieved abroad! Meanwhile, here at home, there would still be his acolytes (Stasyulyevich and Tyutchev) and hangers-on yapping in the company of geniuses such as Malein and Makarov, at the same time continuing to lie low and hide his true nature from prying eyes by keeping at a distance! And all the time putting on an act as a friend and a patriot – in short, doing everything he needed to do. And there you have Turgenev the cosmopolitan! All you have to do is to take a closer look at him, listen to his propaganda both from his own mouth and from the press, and you cannot fail to understand his aversion to and contempt for the Russian way of life and its mores – in effect, Russian life itself, i.e. Russian life as it is lived by progressive people. Of course, you can't expect someone to be a jingoistic patriot and love ugliness at the same time. But the fact remains that practically everything he has done is *hardly any more despicable than what quietly puts a mirthless grin on his face* – or sometimes even openly, as in the case of *Smoke*. Behind this cosmopolitan pose of his lie petty and distasteful objectives.

No matter how little the loss of my work may mean for Russian literature – that is to say the significance of my novels – the fact remains that depriving a Russian novelist of this significance and conferring it on a foreigner is, in my view (not my doing, of course), something for which neither Turgenev nor his accomplices can be forgiven. Russian literature is in any case not so plentiful, and to reduce it even further is a great sin, a betrayal. Added to this is the fact that he, after putting himself in a false position detrimental to Russian literature and recruiting others in his cause, should have been the one to boost contemporary Russian literature in those literary circles – which he dismissed as of no account, unworthy of serious attention, while of course excluding himself from that censure. "There is no point in living there – there's no one." So he left for the place where there was enlightenment, art and life! We were nothing but barbarians or a "Japan"– or, in the words of one of the Goncourt brothers relayed by Grigorovich (Turgenev having introduced them to one other), "*La Russie – c'est le Japon*".* Who was it who went round spreading this slander about Russia? The very same person who had purloined whatever he could of its literature that was unknown to the French and run off with it! And he simply had to talk about me to Auerbach, for example, as he was now doing to the French, giving away what belonged to me.

That is why I have written down *everything that happened between him and me*. But you don't have to take my word for it. How exactly my writings will be used I cannot foretell. If at all possible, I wish I had stopped things getting this far. At the end of this manuscript I will append another comment, in which I will ask in what circumstances, *in what extreme circumstances*, I will permit its use. It is my hope that a man's posthumous wishes will be scrupulously honoured, especially if his dying wish is to avoid causing harm, if only in his own defence, to anyone else – even if it's deserved!

I shall now turn to the question of *who, how and why* some people assisted Turgenev in his dirty work. I can only repeat that he would never have been able to do it all on his own. If he hadn't been told about the chapters of *Malinovka* I had read to people as my work was proceeding, there would not have been any *Fathers and Children*, *Smoke* or *The Country House on the Rhine*, although there might have been a *Sentimental Education* – something that was clearly based on *Malinovka* which was then ready for publication. It was a plain and simple "parallel" text, practically a copy: all it needed was to dress all the dramatis personae in French clothing, etc.

So who was it then who helped him to undermine me, and why? Even now I am not sure of all the details, and I have only recently, over the last two or three years, been able to figure out most of them – although not all. I have something to say about what I have seen and come to realize. The rest will be filled in by others, some by the guilty parties themselves and their associates, and some by eyewitnesses.

Both the general public and the writers themselves are perfectly aware that the authorities will be paying particular attention to them. It is even said that, in the archives of the Third Section, there is a register containing profiles of individuals listed in alphabetical order with a record of their activities. These people and their movements, who they meet and where they meet, are under surveillance; note is taken of their conversations and their political leanings. The writers in particular are watched, since, as a result of the censorship, nothing can be deduced from their published writings and newspaper articles. The problem is that although those whose job it is to keep them under observation – people such as the princes Orlov, Dolgorukov and Dubbelt,* and other generals – are not stupid, and even intelligent in their own way, they are not really of a literary cast of mind and unfamiliar with contemporary trends in European thought and generally out of touch with the mood of our country, so they have tended to think of intellectuals as people with long hair, whiskers and beard and with distinctive tailoring – seeing these as the hallmarks of a liberal. They have judged people by the way they spoke, and above all by whether they have read forbidden books – of which there have been an enormous number: Proudhon* was mentioned only on the quiet; Macaulay, Mignet and even Guizot were taboo!* I frequented the Belinsky circle, as I have mentioned, where, albeit discreetly, we talked about anything and everything (something I still do) uninhibitedly, and castigated harsh measures. Belinsky welcomed anything new or novel that possessed a spark of intelligence or freshness as well as a touch of truth, or was well intentioned. He was quite open about this, and some of us, such as Panayev, openly trumpeted the fact. He – together with everyone who visited Belinsky in fact – was known to the government, as were all the members of his circle. For the most part I shared their views – the emancipation of the serfs, for example, better measures for the enlightenment of society and the people – and I opposed all constraints and limitations on progress, etc. But my head was never turned by youthful utopianism or by the social spirit of equality, brotherhood and that kind of thing the young were so excited about. I never had any faith in materialism or all the benefits which people liked to believe flowed from it – the notion that it would somehow lead to a glorious future for mankind. My attitude to authority was the same as that of the majority of the Russian people – although of course I never hypocritically supported arbitrary rule or draconian measures, or anything of the sort.

They must have known this – and, as I now believe, they were fully aware of my moderate views (after all, I was not a boy, but a grown man of thirty-six). For my part, I felt entirely at ease, just as I have always lived a quiet life without any fear of being watched. When my talent first came to be recognized – and when as a result I had become totally absorbed in my artistic and literary projects – I had no ambition other than to be left alone to live my own life quietly. Even as a child, being of nervous disposition, I avoided crowds, noise and meeting new people. My dream was not that of Trappist silence, but rather the moderation of a Horace – just enough to earn my keep and write and a tight circle of close friends. That is why people later identified me with "Oblomovism".

I became above all addicted to the pen. Writing was my passion. But I had to work as a matter of necessity (even becoming a censor later on, for my sins). I travelled round the world, needing to do something to make a living! And all of this took me away from my writing and my snug little nest.

Of course, the ultraconservative party, which occupied important posts in the administration, could not fail to see that I was not the type to be carried away and allow youthful enthusiasm or extremist ideas of "progress" to go to my head, nor to shrink from progress as such – in short, I was nothing more than a normal man of my times. The year 1855 saw the beginning of reform, and I, of course, applauded this and still now bless the hand that accomplished it. But belonging as I did to a small circle of people, I spent most of my time exclusively with writers, and was naturally well aware what was going on in that milieu and of the ideas of freedom being spread here and in Moscow by Belinsky, Herzen, Granovsky and by literary circles as a whole – ideas which were being circulated in society and among the general population by the press – and of how these fertile and beneficial seeds were being sown and nurtured far and wide to prepare the soil for reform, how literature itself made it easier for the authorities to carry out the first great reform, the emancipation of the serfs, preparing people's minds, putting landowners to shame, spreading ideas of human rights and so on. All this I observed from below, and, of course, repeatedly expressed the thought that literature was doing a great service to the Tsar and to the country. The credit for this belongs, of course, to the Great Reformer,* since without him a dozen literatures could have accomplished nothing. Furthermore, the emperor, Nikolai Pavlovich,* who of course had never read Belinsky, Herzen or Granovsky (or so people said), had convened a meeting of the leaders of the nobility and apprised them of his thinking on the subject of emancipation. The French revolution of 1848 did nothing to lend momentum to this movement, and it was the reign of Tsar Alexander that launched the second great period of reform (after Peter).* It was he who was the innovator.

This has always been my view, and I pay tribute to this heroic figure of our time who left his mark on an entire era not through military glory following the example of others, but through the glory of peace, which he devoted his life, his reign and the power of Russia to preserving! There followed the rule of law, freedom of the press and the "zemstvo",* the election of local councils – something which would have taken the reign of ten tsars to bring about. He did it by himself – and Russia blessed him! I never had the opportunity or the possibility, and the occasion never arose, to mention it anywhere in print. And in any case did this colossus really need our feeble praise or blame? All this was so far removed from me! But, as I have so often said, as far as the tiny literary service (that is to say, any influence on people's minds) is concerned, my silence (which may have seemed deliberate) regarding major issues that were way above my head and beyond my scope was, I later discovered, interpreted by those who were so obligingly keeping tabs on me as some kind of protest, if not a revolt, and turned the conservative party against me!

On one occasion, when I was reading my intended but never published 'Foreword' to a separate edition of *Malinovka*, A.G. Troynitsky,* a friend of the minister of internal affairs and a close acquaintance of mine, told me that I was being "too complimentary to Belinsky and literature and crediting him with too much influence on people's minds". In this foreword, I did in fact go into some detail concerning how and in what way literature and Belinsky's article had helped the government – not to mention, of course, that it was the latter that had taken the initiative in, and deserves the credit for, the reform. It is really not necessary or appropriate for me to mention this. So that is why I refrained from taking up my pen and intervening in something where I genuinely had nothing useful to say. Furthermore, I hardly ever referred, either in writing or when talking to others, to the so-called "uppermost" class of society – and for a perfectly simple reason: *I knew absolutely nothing about it* and had never come into contact with it.

I had enough good sense and self-respect not to poke my nose in where I was not wanted – because of my birth and financial means. As you know, the conservatives commend England as a country, because everyone there knows their place – and that is a very good thing! A lord is a lord and everyone treats him as such; a shopkeeper is a shopkeeper; artists and writers know their status – and so on.

I acted accordingly, and was right to do so. What's more, I was of a nervous disposition, and rather shy. Both my inclinations and my tastes confined me to my study and a small, intimate circle of friends. But the ultraconservatives saw this in a different light: partly as bad manners and lack of respect for authority, and partly as overweening pride, and that was why I shunned the conservatives. But neither did I stubbornly and wilfully distance myself from them: when the occasion arose for me to associate with them, I was more than happy to do so, if I felt that there was any affinity between us, and I am on friendly terms with some of them.

I was beginning to be watched more closely, in order to detect my political leanings. Was I liberal, democrat or conservative? Was I genuinely religious? Or did I go to church so that I could show... what? And to whom?

Now, with all this indifference to religion, secular values on the contrary practically require you to conceal your religiousness, something which progressives equate with stupidity. So the question arises: for whose benefit am I dissembling? The authorities? But they too benefit from a wide range of abilities and functions, and are no longer bothered by whether or not people go to church, fast or take Communion. And that is a good thing, since, in religion, freedom is more important than in any other area of life. There was absolutely nothing that I was in search of – quite the contrary; I was frightened and full of anxiety, and it was with some misgiving that I accepted a welcome and flattering invitation from V.P. Titov* to tutor the late tsarevich* in literature temporarily, until another tutor could be found to replace the previous one who had fallen ill. Afterwards I felt afraid and lost confidence because of my lack of teaching experience and expertise, and shuddered to think of the responsibility I was assuming in this important position, and with great regret I backed out.

There were many who, unaware of my nervous temperament, also put this down perhaps to a lack of sympathy for those who were liked by everybody, including myself. Can one really read the heart of another? If people could look into my heart, they would see something quite appalling! If, however, my unsociability and reclusiveness were attributed to my Oblomov-type laziness, I would have nothing to say – but who cares! Rather than putting everything down to my "laziness", it would be much better to talk about my "artistic, contemplative" temperament, which naturally leads me to live an inner life of creativity, intellectual endeavour and, above all, imagination, which goes hand in hand with an aversion to crowds. All this is exacerbated by the nervousness and timidity I have already referred to.

So much for my Oblomovism! It is something that may not be present in everyone, but it is typical of many writers, artists, scholars and intellectuals. Count Lev Tolstoy, Pisemsky, Count Alexei Tolstoy, Ostrovsky, they all have their own little niches – small, tightly knit circles! That is the way things were back in 1858 and '59. It was then that I published *Oblomov*, marking the beginning of my falling-out with Turgenev over his *Nest of the Gentry* and *On the Eve*. It was in 1856, I believe, that I had my *Frigate Pallada* published by the Moscow publisher A.I. Glazunov* – and, of course, I made a point of presenting the first copies to the entire imperial family, with a dedication to Grand Prince Konstantin Nikolayevich,* to whom I was indebted for this voyage. I had no misgivings about this, because this book was, as it were, my compulsive literary account of the voyage. So I had no choice, I was trapped. And for better or for worse, I had no compunction about presenting my work. But when it came to novels, that was another matter. I couldn't even bring myself to show *Oblomov* to my pupil, Grand Prince Nikolai Alexandrovich. After all, who am I to present him with my novel? I'm no Pushkin or Gogol. Who doesn't write novels nowadays? It's as if I think so much of myself that I have written this great book and am therefore entitled to present it to any grandee… I was naive enough to think that when grandees find something good they would want to express their pleasure to the author.

In the old days books would be offered in the hope of receiving a gift, a ring or something: this seemed to me inappropriate – like a form of begging. And in any case the Grand Prince was still a young man, and I didn't even know whether he'd be able to read novels. This was something which sycophants understood and interpreted differently. "He doesn't want it, it would seem, and therefore he won't acknowledge it!" It appeared that quite a crowd of sycophants had gathered – and, my goodness, look what happened! I had never imagined anything like this, of course: it had never occurred to me that people would be interested in me or pay any particular attention to me. I had never suspected that I possessed enough talent to attract the attention of those above me. I had been gratified by the success of *Oblomov* – and even privately had a high opinion of it and showed it to the minister of education. I even thought that he might at some point mention it to the tsar – and that was all! But since he failed to do this and most probably no one higher up had ever heard of it, I couldn't help thinking that it wasn't an important-enough work to carry on promoting it. And going around promoting my work was something I couldn't bring myself to do, especially since I had no idea how these important people felt about literature. In a word, as a nobody, I couldn't make any progress – and that was my undoing.

As I say, it just never occurred to me that the ultraconservative party was aware of my every step, every word and every… letter! They certainly were aware, however (although that wasn't really a problem), and it was on the basis of that knowledge, including my trouble with Turgenev, that they concocted a whole series of tragicomic moves against me, poisoning my life and finding no use for me. But what helped them, helped them a great deal, in all this was my own incautious sharp tongue, together with the frankness of my writing – and, last but not least, Turgenev himself!

My correspondence with him was common knowledge, as was my confrontation with him and my relations with various other people. My fierce reactions to various things and even to people close to me were often spontaneous impulses – that is to say, they often sprang from my instinctive and highly developed intellectual analysis and powers of observation, as well as from that spirit of negativity that has become the prime mover and weapon of our age – everywhere and in all things, but nowhere more than in literature. It was with Gogol that our literature first set out on this negative path, and I don't know when we will work our way to achieving some kind of positive consensus which all of us could settle for. Perhaps never! And that's very depressing. Negativity and analysis have undermined what used to be accepted rules to live by and dethroned authority at all levels, including even moral and intellectual authority; life has become degraded, and morality has been discarded. I don't know what the world is coming to.

My own sensitive, nervous and contemplative temperament has been poisoned by the curse of analysis, yet for all that, at the same time, my heart and much else has remained intact. Nevertheless I have been told that I am behind the times: so be it! I'll do my best to "see it through". Of course, intellectual analysis has not done away with negativity, by which I mean ugliness and falsehood in all areas of life and all levels of society – my tongue was wagging in spite of myself, and I spoke either in jest or too harshly. At the same time, I have never ceased to welcome those very same phenomena and people, acknowledging, as I do, their positive (that is to say, their good) sides. But it is not these sides which are the first things to strike you, but rather the dark sides, the harsh sides – that is why people keep quiet about the former, whereas it is the latter that are noticed and talked about. This was something encountered at every step with others too, but these others were not being followed, and their every word was not being recorded, and that's why they got away with it, whereas my every word was noted, weighed and held against me. "Nothing to worry about!" they said. I'm the first to acknowledge my many failings – one more reason why I don't impose myself on others.

Yet I knew, of course, that the people watching me often became confused, seeing me as a contradictory and inconsistent individual, liable to speak out both for and against the same thing, and as often as not right here, in this very place. I would take a liking to something and then reject it – perfectly understandably! My mind would alight on something, and then my imagination would embellish it with a different colour, while my heart had its own say in the matter. By the next day, however, not a trace would remain: vanished like a mirage!

God knows what kind of psychologist would be able to make sense of such a neurotic temperament! But with their open and often blatant snooping and tracking they tried to wreck my imagination and puzzle out its whims, which they knew nothing about and had no qualms about destroying; all they were good at was to punish and torment me! Why does he do one thing and not another? All they had to do was to leave me in peace, and there wouldn't have been any trouble! I could have got on with my writing, my mind would have been at rest and, as far as possible, I would even have been happy. All they can think of is that I am the dog in the manger. They have put their trust in my envious rival. But this particular "dog" has got its teeth into it and won't let it go. It's hard work, and clouded with doubt, and will take a long time and a lot of persistence, but this dog will see it through. Nothing must be allowed to frustrate that! Yet they are frustrating me and hounding me on all sides; they are ripping everything from me and giving it to others. If you're going to destroy a person's desires, why not kill that person while you're at it? And that's what they've done!

Writing is my calling, and it has become a passion, a passion that has been mine since childhood – since my schooldays. I wrote to my schoolmates, whether they were in my room or not – I wrote to everyone! And I still do, especially in the form of letters. And that's perfectly understandable: the epistolary form doesn't require any preparation or planning, and it's therefore a spontaneous impulse to express oneself, and can be effected on the spot: no persons, characters, details or anything whatsoever to restrain or dampen the free flow of thought and imagination. All that's needed is a correspondent and any subject or idea that interests me or catches my fancy – and that does the trick! I sit down like a musician at the piano and give free rein to my fantasy, a thought or a feeling, untethered and able, in short, to indulge the slightest whim or impulse in my own way – practically just as in life itself. And it is as hard for me to tear myself away from my writing paper as it is for a pianist strumming away on his instrument. A whole evening or morning can pass – the force of the electric current can weaken just as in a Leiden jar. I feel cold, limp, inert until the next day, or the day after. Something will get into me, and I start playing again – or, rather, start writing again – and I come to life. They exploited this and used it against me, tricking me into correspondence and then punishing me for what I had written, if it didn't happen to be to their taste, and playing all kinds of tricks on me and examining me as if I were a corpse. Any play of the imagination, as for example in my correspondence with a woman, they would take as a kind of flirtation – or as an attempt to "seduce" or toy with the affections of some young lady – and use that to torment me!

Sometimes the content of the letter failed to interest me much or at all, but it was enough for them if it played on my nerves – and off I went, writing again!

And they would spend so much time on their cunning, poisonous fantasies! They would twist some of my letters inside out and write back to me, and I would have to answer them.

Or they would try various different handwritings, to make it seem as if the letter had come from some distant place, when in fact my correspondent lived not far away. Sometimes it wasn't the young lady herself who wrote the letter, but someone else. And I was constantly having to reply. Sometimes they tried to arrange meetings abroad, in Paris or Berlin – although, of course, I wouldn't go. But I was still having to write all kinds of nonsense – anything that came into my head! It was, supposedly, just a joke, or it was in fact a genuine expression of jealousy or malice (whatever the circumstances required), but did I really feel passionate or malicious? Or was I joking and pretending? If so, I would pay for it!

I thought that these "rivals" for the affections of the lady in question would get back at me for misunderstanding the real nature of these letters. And I carried on writing, passing it all off as a joke! But this only irritated them even more, for which they punished me by making things very difficult for me – and not just with the letters. So I gave up, started to retreat, explaining that I was an author by nature and that I often assumed the role of an author without meaning to, and that I found it difficult to explain where the author stopped and the human being began. I assured them, the women (and the priest who was sent to see me), that I was not by any means playing a game or joking when I wrote that I felt I can do perfectly well without women, and so on – and finally that, with Raisky, I was striving to work out and explain how a man with imagination could comprehend, when he is an artist by nature, what others feel by experience.

All of this, of course (namely, this pointless writing), is a kind of "Oblomovism"! But the truth is, as I tried to show in *Oblomov*, that "Oblomovism", like so much else in life, isn't something that happens through any fault of our own, but for a whole host of independent reasons. It was all around us like the air itself, and prevented (and is still preventing) me from sticking firmly to my chosen calling, as I would have been able to do in England, France or Germany.

There was no clear-cut literary path for us to tread, and we set foot on it only tentatively and fearfully, almost by accident. It was all right, of course, for those of us with means who could concentrate single-mindedly on their work. But for the rest of us it meant fragmenting our time and attention! The things I had to do! All that time spent in the office just for a crust of bread – in "the course of my official duties" I even had to travel round the world "to review our North American colonies", as my official record put it! Was it any more than a painstaking accumulation of the sum total of my thoughts, feelings, observations and experience, and imagination, and including them in my carefully considered works? In any case, in spite of all the obstacles and impediments, I succeeded in completing six or seven volumes. In another manuscript, ('To My Critics'), I explained why I had taken so long to write my novels. It was, to quote Belinsky, because I had packed so much into each of them that it "would have been" – and actually was – "enough for ten shorter ones". It is in fact amazing that I was able to write them in spite of all the obstacles! Envy alone took a tremendous toll! She kept a relentless grip on me to this day, never relaxing. She is intent on continuing to do so and on exchanging places with me. She is constantly reminding me of this, while I, in order to protect myself against the lies and slander, have felt obliged *bon gré, mal gré*,* with the greatest repugnance, to write this account.

I still have this faint hope that, if Envy is content with the damage she has already done and is willing to leave me in peace without raking over old coals, I will be able to tear up these pages.

This was not the way I wanted to tell this story, but rather by writing a whole new work, but my age, I repeat, the cooling of the blood, and this whole struggle has impeded me in my creative endeavour, the whole painful process of creating characters and images – images placed in their appropriate settings and so on. And even if I do put pen to paper, Turgenev will lose no time in stealing "parallels" from my work and circulating them to all and sundry abroad, while doing his best to prevent my work being translated. In any case, as long as I carry on writing, his numerous acolytes will continue to eavesdrop and spy on me and report to him beforehand, and he will keep on stealing my work for his own purposes and for circulation to others. Meanwhile Envy, far from sleeping, is planning further vengeance. In the current issue of *Vestnik Evropy* there is a vapid story by Turgenev entitled 'The Watch', with a footnote announcing a major new novel.

Turgenev himself is not capable of writing a major novel, and I have the feeling that he has once again concocted a kind of "parallel" from my letters – by extracting, that is to say, an idea from them and creating a character based on this idea. He will then announce: "Here you are – a major new work from me! And Goncharov has written nothing, so obviously all that's been published recently is my own work – and not his!" Perhaps I'm mistaken though, and he has come up with something of his own!

As for the letters, I have to confess that I have been somewhat naive. Of course, like everyone else, I knew that all letters which are posted are opened by the post office – that is pretty well an open secret, but in my naivety I thought that this applied only to suspicious characters who were under scrutiny, and that all the other letters, even if they were opened by mistake, would be disregarded. In fact I thought that letters written by people who were not troublemakers, who were reliable, harmless, not suspect in any way, were *sacrosanct and inviolable – not only by the authorities* (or so I was naive enough to believe), *but also by the humblest post-office employees*, who were the ones who opened the letters! I thought that normally they would be accustomed to sorting the letters, and would therefore know, on the basis of the handwriting and addresses, which ones to open and which not to open, and also, of course, that they would respect the sentiments and words of others, just as they would abstain from rifling their pockets and cases, when they know who is writing to whom, that is to say when there is nothing that would be of interest to the secret police. This respect for personal privacy, affairs, interests, relationships, thoughts and speech, I considered, and continue to consider, not only *the binding and absolutely essential moral duty of honest people*, but also *the standard practice of the highest national authorities.*

Anyone who violates this obligation can only inspire fear and disgust, rather than respect. Naturally, when I tossed my improvised letters into the post box every day, I did so confident in the knowledge that, although one or two letters might happen to be opened by mistake, a scrupulous gentleman would refrain from reading them out of sheer decency, and even if at times he happened to read one, that wouldn't be so terrible: after all, he wouldn't be likely to go around blabbing about the fact that he had been so nosy as to read someone else's letter. I wasn't particularly worried, in any case, because I knew that a number of my correspondents would have read them, so that it wouldn't make much difference if some post-office workers happened to read them by mistake! But, as I later discovered, many of my letters were received and read by people to whom they were not addressed. But what was worse was the fact that unscrupulous use was made of them, in flagrant violation of my rights – not to mention my property! Once again, it was Turgenev who was behind this scandalous behaviour! I happen to have one of his letters where he writes *"que c'est une calamité publique que je n'écris pas"*.* What he was trying to do, in other words, was to provoke me into corresponding with him, in order to milk not only my books for material, but even my actual thoughts, on the same old grounds that I was being a dog in the manger! "What a nerve!" If you can't dredge up your own material, then don't try to write, or just write what you can. It's not enough for him to become the Russian Teniers or Ostade.* Write historical overviews, if you must, but of other countries! However that may be, those letters found their way to him and others, especially after I had begun to suspect the existence of all these machinations. Then, in order to divert suspicion from Turgenev and themselves, they started to supply other authors as well with the contents. Of course, at his instigation, nothing that I had written should somehow not be allowed to disappear. So he cunningly arranged things with the police to ensure that none of my literary projects should escape his attention. Like a spider, he was delicately and subtly spinning his web!

In this way Turgenev controlled this entire gang of people not only to extract material from me, but, more importantly, to keep himself constantly *au courant** with everything I was thinking, doing and writing! What he particularly feared and worried about was that I might be writing a new novel. Craftily spreading the lie that he was not the one "borrowing" from me, but that it was I who was "borrowing" from him, and that it was I who was envious of him instead of the other way round, he, as was later explained to me, became the victim of his own envy, and thus arranged to create a whole network of accomplices. He persuaded them, through his lies, to do his bidding and ensure that he, together with Auerbach, would be supplied with copies of my writings, thus providing him with material for his own future stories as well as Auerbach's *Country House on the Rhine*. These people who were taken in by his lies should, of course, have been furious with my envious rival and sympathetic to his "victim". They felt they owed their duty to him and forgot the old wise saying, *audiatur et altera pars.** It was easy for Turgenev to persuade them that I had been the one who had "borrowed" from him, because the whole novel *à peu près** had already been known to him, so that he was naturally able to tell them in advance what I would be writing and claim it for himself. If he hadn't been helped, *Smoke*, *The Country House on the Rhine* and other works would never have been written. In a letter I might, for example, just happen to mention casually the idea for a plot, and he, sniffing around as he always was, would follow the scent and seize the morsel and promptly regurgitate it, leaving me to appear to be imitating him! But this was not his worst abuse of my letters: there was even worse to come! If I ever happened to respond too strongly or incautiously, he would exploit the opportunity to the full, and the consequences for me could be disastrous!

I would be forced to give up everything – my employment,* my small circle of friends, among which I could find shelter – and hide, so to speak, from the outside world! And to this I must add that thanks to these letters, as well as to my writings, they would often begin to play their usual tricks on me and torment me! For example, certain ladies and gentlemen would act out roles from my novels with me; sometimes it would be Olga, Nadenka or Vera, with me playing the parts of Aduyev, Oblomov and Raisky, among others! Why? Well, you had better ask those who thought up the idea! What fun it must have been: "You are supposed to be talented, naive" – and even that was thought to be so comical! All this started off on a small scale, in private among just a few people. It was clever of them; obviously they had a lot of resources at their disposal, and plenty of time… Suddenly they would send a nephew of mine from the provinces (I had four nephews) to work here, as in *The Same Old Story*. Or they would get some woman or other to speak the words of Olga or Vera, and so on. "I mean, after all, you toy with us as characters in your letters, so we'll have some fun with you!" Incidentally, this farce began long ago – before any letters! But even letters that I had written long ago to members of my family were brazenly opened and read! So, you see, I was right when I mentioned earlier that everything that happened to me could only have happened in Russia. And if Turgenev, if only for the fact that he saw and knew what was being done (and is still being done) to me, went abroad, then he would have been right to do so, especially if he had not taken any stolen goods with him!

To explain why all this was being done – and done so painstakingly and consistently as to be worthy of a better cause – well, it's simply beyond me! There is this book – *Mystificateurs et mystifiés (Bibliophile Jacob) par Michel Raymond*.* Read it! It describes a gang of pranksters just before the revolution of the Eighties and Nineties in France. It's a historical document, and from it you can get an idea of the mores, education and nature of the society in the course of its growth and development! It irked them that I cherished my little nook and my tiny morsel of poetic independence and wanted to share the gifts that talent, education and nature had chosen to bestow on me! Furthermore, if I possess some talent – and my letters have been appreciated by their readers – then... then why should I have been tormented and persecuted like that? I would have thought that instead I should have been encouraged in one way or another in what I was doing. For one thing, people shouldn't have sided with Turgenev in his campaign against me, or eavesdropped and copied my writings for him.

My writings were all my own work, and without all these impediments and all the support he was getting, my novels would have stayed in Russia. And if they were such that even forgeries of them attracted attention in foreign literary circles, then people's respect for Russian literature would of course have increased. "My word! What importance you attach to your scribblings!" I will be told. "Isn't it just as well that three little books would be published here in Russian and abroad: Russia wouldn't be the worse for it! You must have a very high opinion of yourself..."

No, it wasn't me, but Turgenev himself who, in the very same spirit, rated my work very highly. Belinsky and Dobrolyubov, of course, would both have appreciated my work, but they were no longer around. Turgenev alone in his particular way was a refined critic of art, and no others of that older generation were still around. But journalism and practical utility have now taken over and ousted belles-lettres. What I am saying is the literal truth. So if there is anything novel and original in my books, then taking it from us here in Russia and exporting it is not so much a loss for Russia itself, but rather for Russian belles-lettres! "Well, it's not all that bad," people will say. "It's not a total loss! It all started with Chernyshevsky,* and the current generation of Russian publicists still share that view."

In my opinion there should be room for both!

People will say that if they fantasized about me in that way, wilfully failing to distinguish between my life and my fiction and turning them into one big laughing stock, then it may very well be that this business of stealing my work and handing it over to someone else was all part of a prank, as in the case of the character of Oblomov, whom they first savaged and then came to terms with, making it up to him and reassuring him. It was probably something like that! They ganged up on him, robbed him, gave away his property and never returned it. These were two separate moves: taking away and giving away, and for this two separate teams were necessary. Meanwhile, that other man, taking advantage of the situation, took it all abroad with him and made a big show of it, keeping part of the spoils for himself and giving the rest away to foreigners. A bad joke! Either (and here I'm still guessing) all this was carefully planned in order to force me to write a new book, thus proving that "you were really the source drawn upon by all those thirsting for ideas and images". "Write!" was the demand constantly being made of me. "Aren't you writing anything new?" "Too late, too late!" Ruin some dealer who has been amassing capital for sixty years and tell him to make another pile – but he can't! And meanwhile he is supposed to be writing! Restore his lost energy, stimulate his imagination, force him to relive his life of artistic endeavour when he has lost the will to live at all. To make him write would require other diametrically opposed resources: you shouldn't have clipped his wings!

Even though I want nothing more than to sit down quietly with my arms folded! And I am constantly surprised when I am so often asked whether or not I am writing. Everyone I meet attaches so much importance to that! Why, from the very beginning – or if not from the beginning, then from the publication of *Oblomov* in 1859 – did hostilities against me begin? It was either the censorship banning the publication of any article in my favour, or the hiding from me of any favourable impression made anywhere by my novel, etc. All this became more and more noticeable. But why? Why all this hostility, all these dirty tricks? It's such a nuisance to have to put up with all this – it's the bane of my life, and it saddens me to try to think of the possible reasons for some of the misunderstandings of which I am the victim...

The crux of the matter, I repeat, is that the representatives of the ultraconservative party, in their blind pursuit of their own interests, have looked on (and apparently continue to look on) my unsociability, my contemplative cast of mind, my creative concerns, my need to be left in peace, my seclusion, my remaining above the fray, my indifference to what is going on around me – in other words my nervous, artistic temperament – and they see it all as a wilful disdain for conventional norms of the official standards of the Russian way of life, as proof of arrogance, if you please, as a refusal to recognize the various authorities...

And it is not as if Turgenev had no hand in all this! He, as I was to realize later, cunningly misrepresented me as an out-and-out opponent, practically an enemy, of all the highest authorities. In so doing, he aroused the suspicions and hostility of the highest conservative circles against me, thereby facilitating his ruthless theft of my manuscripts and letters.

Furthermore, in that passage in the history of Russian literature by Courrière (which he himself, of course, wrote, aided and abetted by that Frenchman, praising himself the whole time), he portrayed me as *an enemy of despotism and scourge of the Russian government*, among other sly, slanderous comments. Thus began his campaign of persecution, the watching, the spying in order to keep tabs on me. And the moment I expressed myself too freely in conversation or criticized any government action – the kind of thing that is being said by anyone at any time – all this was taken down and held in evidence against me. And, of course, retribution soon followed – every day and at every step I took – and when all those sycophants and people spying on me, dogging my footsteps to keep me under surveillance, became confused when I failed to act as they expected, they put it down to Oblomovian laziness and pressed on with their campaign of intimidation, vexing me by acting out scenes from *Oblomov* and other novels. According to them, I was just describing myself. "Well, in that case," I said to them, "why are you still bothering me like this and picking on me like a bunch of schoolboys, if, using your words, I was 'describing myself'? Just leave me alone – this has already cost me so much pain!"

But there was really no point in talking to this obsessive crowd of people. They saw nothing in me except Oblomov, Aduyev and Raisky – and they wore me out! But they continued hounding me, if only because *when I was a civil servant I did not directly and unequivocally serve the ultraconservative cause in my writings, and also because I did not forthrightly condemn radicalism, and in my newspaper articles and novels I did not excoriate nihilism or support the fundamental tenets of the social order, religion, the family, the government and so on.* And all this caused me a lot of trouble. Turgenev had begun with *A Nest of the Gentry*, and they helped him to complete the rest. No one in that camp had even suspected that I had long since started *to go my own way, serving the cause as an artist* – and had even placed my *Malinovka* within a liberal context in *Vestnik Evropy*, where it was accepted only after a lot of grumbling and grimacing. In the novel I had supported respect for religion in the character of Vera, as well as undermining radicalism in the character of Volokhov – and the fallen women were redeemed by their suffering. In the final analysis, the novel was written sincerely and with conviction – and, what's more, *disinterestedly*!

No one understood that the young extremists themselves were probably upset with me for, as they saw it, being unfair to the younger generation by representing Volokhov in a bad (that is to say, unflattering) light! The older generation were upset because I had been *too soft* on him – in other words, I hadn't torn him to pieces. But I had done neither of these things. All I had done was to paint a portrait of him as I saw him, which, in fact, was the secret of its success, precisely as a portrait! If I had written a polemic or had painted an unflattering or crude picture, it would have been a disaster! In a polemic I would have appeared even feebler than some smart newspaper journalist. If I had invested the portrait with any trace of my own indignation, it would have seemed that I was taking sides – which would have been totally out of place.

People forget that an artist charts his own course and manner, and that his motto is *sine ira*.*

"No! You must be favourably disposed towards radicalism, if you don't take him to task and you're not angry with him at all!" I'm not angry with him: I'm painting a portrait of him as I see him and as he is reflected in my imagination. And therein, and only therein, lies my strength. And I cannot ever, ever write for a set of prescribed ideas! (In the manuscript 'To My Critics' I explain this in detail.)

Frankly, I am surprised by the childish attempts of the conservative party to defend their fundamental principles of respect for religion, authority, morality and so on in literature! The *Moskovskie Vedomosti*,* i.e. Katkov, it is true, successfully opposed the propaganda of Herzen, Ogarev, Bakunin* and others at precisely the time when these gentlemen, after relinquishing all ties with Russia and unaware of what was going on there and what exactly it needed following the reforms of which they were the most enthusiastic proponents, abandoned their former positive positions by pointing at the squalor of Russian public life and the administration – something which proved highly successful, and which started to confuse our younger generation by advocating the extreme and ruthless negation by the last remnants of Parisian gutter philosophy and politics which had survived one crisis after another. They tried to impose upon us their own feverish lifestyle, with its never-ending transient, spasmodic aberrations and impulses, which we do not share. Finally, they stood up for Poland, to the detriment of our own nation's interests, even though it meant alienating their true friends in this country. Katkov was the first to expose vigorously the lying propaganda which had taken root in the fertile soil of the minds of the rising generation, which needed a strict system of methodical and solid education. And Katkov succeeded in winning great popularity. But the moment he became an official, although unannounced, guardian of conservative interests, he was suspected of partiality, sycophancy and unsavoury self-interest, and his popularity gradually began to wane.

It's easy to understand why. Our government is strong; its strength does not derive from any given party, but from the trust and devotion of the people as a whole. But what Katkovs would be able to support or defend it! It is too well protected – so much so that it is difficult, although sometimes necessary in the public interest, to speak out against it in the press. It can defend itself from the literary standpoint in only one direct way: by means of the official index magazine and refuting false rumours and malicious gossip, and by offering a dignified defence of its views, actions and intentions whenever the occasion arises. And that's all! And this is what is being done with regard to foreign policy, for example, by the *Journal de Saint-Pétersbourg** when it analyses pan-European political questions on which Russia can state its views. As a result, our government can no longer dictate to the press what it can print. All it can do is ban whatever it deems harmful. Literary officials in its pay never do any good – all they can do is undermine trust in the actions of the government. Pretending to be sincere won't work: they'll find you out, however much you try to hide from them. France and England are no examples here. There can be quite open opposition in England, since it exercises restraint on the government by criticism, and after an electoral victory the opposition itself becomes the government. In France there are rival parties, each supporting its claim to power.

It is understandable therefore that in both countries different bodies and institutions are possible and necessary, each supporting its own party and competing with one another. This could never happen in our country. Here everyone must support the government and the prevailing religion, and any dissent is deemed a crime. In our country everyone has to be a conservative, and the role of the government is to exercise oversight (a function it performs diligently) over those who, in the press, dare to deviate, however slightly. This is the only leeway permitted to the newspapers, while the government acts as the shepherd whose job it is to prevent the sheep from straying too far. But there is nowhere for them to go!

What then is left for these compliant newspapers to advocate? That we must pray to God, respect authority, and all that. But everyone knows this. Foreign newspapers have a different role. Some are in business to demonstrate that France will prosper once more with the advent of Chambord,* while others champion the House of Orléans. Others again argue that the Napoleonic dynasty alone can save France. In England, the opposition press dogs the footsteps of every government and seizes on every mistake, while the government defends itself in its own newspapers. And the government and the rest of the country are stronger precisely because of this open control! This only goes to show that there is an urgent necessity also for a government-controlled press in order to provide an alternative to the free liberal press which the censorship has not managed to gag! But what about us?

Well, we will be told that society is being penetrated by so-called *destructive forces* – the weakening grip of religion, authority, the family and so on. But consider the increasing influence in the West of what is known as the propaganda of internationalism, which calls for anarchy and the total destruction of the old order!

Yes, we must face the fact that something strange, almost unprecedented, at least in terms of magnitude, is happening in the general conceptions of mankind. It is of profound and worldwide proportions! But against the narrow, selfish radicalism of half-baked youths, and against the party of the sans-culottes, society is armed with common sense, maturity and every other asset – moral, intellectual and material – and is capable of halting the rising tide of this ugly extreme radicalism. Against the extreme manifestations of this evil, this latter-day version of highway robbery, everyone is up in arms. And neither the commune, the pathological product of a diseased imagination, nor sheer malevolence and unbridled passions will ever overcome the healthy majority of humanity, in just the same way that a gang of escaped jailbirds will never prevail against an entire city. The danger does not lie here. But what needs to be done about the loss of respect for what used to be considered sacred, inviolable and essential, and the moral standard which once governed the conduct of human society? An analysis of the age injected realism into spiritual, moral and intellectual life, the universal and inexorable verification of everything existing in nature, in things and in human beings, seeking through intelligence and science to triumph over nature. Everything is inexorably subject to analysis: our innermost feelings, our highest aspirations, our precious secrets and the mysteries of the human soul – the entire activity of our spiritual nature, with its passions, dreams and poetry. The imperfect analysis of science and experience has left nothing untouched. Honour, honesty, nobility of spirit, moral refinement in all its forms, can be reduced to the practical level of policing. Our sentiments – and in general all the good and bad manifestations of our psychology – come down to laws governed by our nervous system.

Reasoning and its functions are nothing but mechanical, and are not driven by free will. Man is therefore blameless, neither good nor bad. He is just the product and victim of the laws of necessity, written nowhere, but simply imposed by blind nature, having nothing to do with God or the concept of some universal force. This is, *à peu près*, the message to the past from the most up-to-date thinkers of our age. Youth is thrilled by this glow, and rushes headlong towards the flames. The older generations are bewildered – and the fruit of this realism is universal suspense, as we wonder how the riddle of this latter-day sphinx will be solved and how mankind will be recompensed for what it has lost.

Man, life and science are in a state of dissolution and disorder: the task now takes on the form of a frenzied struggle, and what the outcome will be no one knows. The phenomenon is working itself out, and we are living in the epicentre of this turmoil and in the heat of this momentous clash – the end is not in sight, and we have no way of knowing what will happen.

But prolonged waiting leaves us in a state of exhaustion and *indifference*. And it is *indifference* that we must struggle to overcome. But we possess neither the moral nor the material weapons to do so! Indifference is a foe which offers no resistance; it remains silent, sinking slowly out of sight, like mercury in a thermometer. Because of this indifference, a thousand-year-old papacy has been lost from view. As a result, Christians are groaning under the Turkish yoke, and Christian Europe is helping the Herzegovinians instead of a new pan-European crusade in diplomatic dress.

Sentiment was banished long ago from public and national life, and finally from private and intimate matters, and was replaced in its turn by such things as compromise and so on.

Perhaps, or even probably, all this will pass, just as the air clears after a storm – and then there will be a fire from which a phoenix arises, and a fresh, newly cleansed life will be reborn with less balm, feeling and passion, but more truth and order than in the past.

After all, if everything is to be broken up, then of course we are entitled to expect such a result, otherwise what has all this smoke been for?

Or, when the nightmare is over, man will awake from it, refreshed after such an ordeal, healthier and more intelligent – and will return to that same unexpected, mysterious and hard life of suffering, and once again retrieve only the good things from the ashes, the good things which have been cast aside by relentless innovators, and place them back where they belong, and man will come to believe in them and cherish them even more, conscientiously and with understanding. May God grant that! I believe that this will happen!

But let me now turn to this "indifference" which I have just referred to. Neither tendentious conservative journals nor tendentious novels and articles written to order will make things better – none of the issues of our time can be resolved on the basis of the predilections of ourselves or others, but rather on the basis of science and experience, that is to say the facts and the times, but not necessarily the present. When I see the childish attempts of certain writers championing the cause of the upper classes, or family unity, or a given religion, and writing stories and novels on the subject, what surprises me is not that they are campaigning against the current chemical decomposition of life (like children playing with toy soldiers), but rather the fact that the conservatives believe in the possibility of their success! They include highly talented people such as Leskov.* But he is no help. I have read what he has written and enjoyed his lively style (*The Diary of an Archpriest*),* and the masterly scenes from the life of the clergy or Old Believers (*The Sealed Angel*).*

I have read hardly anything by Prince Meshchersky,* except one or two passages here and there. What he writes is not bad on the whole, and pretty good in parts. But it is said that these kinds of books are read by the upper classes (that is to say, those who have a personal interest in them), and they, especially Meshchersky, so I have heard, hang portraits of that circle, make mischief, spread rumours and that sort of thing. And that's their only effective action. Their efforts have no literary clout or effect on society at large, because they lack any clear-cut goal or direction, and above all any creativity. Therefore, for these two reasons, there is no enthusiasm, and hence no influence, no lesson to be learnt or example to be followed as is the case, for example, with the novels of Count Leo Tolstoy (*Anna Karenina*). Readers enjoy Count Leo Tolstoy's artistry, his keen analysis; they are indifferent to high society because, like a true, straightforward artist, he too is indifferent to it, and for that reason his high-society characters are simply people like any others, that is to say, educated people. Count Tolstoy's effect on his readers is that of a poet, a creative person, and with the same skill and authorial commitment he can depict peasants, woods, fields and even dogs, not to mention the salons of the capital and their socialites. And the reader follows him with the same delight, hardly noticing that he is reading about the aristocracy with the same detachment as the author himself! In articles in the so-called "protective" journals attempts to interest the reader in the question of religion or respect for family ties and so on do have an effect on those who have not abandoned or changed their convictions about the subject, but those who remain sceptical, matter-of-fact and in denial don't even read them, or pour scorn on them, especially if they still suspect these efforts on the part of journalists to be insincere – which for the most part they really are. Their objectives are thought to be anything but altruistic!

So this "conservative" party apparently also takes me to task for not playing the game and not coming out unequivocally against radicalism. But I have done my part, as a writer and an artist, with my portrait of Volokhov, as well as depicting "Granny" as the prototype of the conservative Russian – what more do they want?

There is no longer any need to speak out against radicalism: it's dismissed out of hand, it was short-lived!

As to inveighing against "indifference" on any issue, idea, feeling or tendency, I can't, I'm at the end of my tether. I could wield the pen not as a journalist, but as a novelist – something which you "protectors" tore from my grasp and gave away to another. And what did that "other" do for you, in return for this "protection"? Both openly and covertly he bared his teeth at Russia and at all of you and tried to ingratiate himself with the younger generation (unsuccessfully however: they saw through him) and sing the national anthem with some Lunins and Baburins* or other, while at the same time knocking at the opposite door with his article 'What We Sent', and ending up by becoming a French literary figure and distributing piecemeal the accomplishments of Russian literature.

And you made me a kind of scapegoat for the overall demoralization, the loss of fundamental beliefs and feelings in society, as well as for the indifference to the religious and political authorities and to family values!

Why blame me for all that? These are values that I cherish and continue to believe in. I look at life and live it in my own way, and have done all I could. Now I want to take a rest and live out my life in peace.

"No, you must write!" people will yell at me.

But who will listen to me, when I have been robbed of what significance I had? Mind you, I'm no genius. If I were to write, I wouldn't transform people's ideas and convictions. All that could be said of me was that I could be labelled a tendentious writer, and I would not be left in peace even in my old age – not that I actually enjoy much peace now!

"Leave me alone!" I will say. "I am an artist, a scholar, a person to whom God has granted a creative talent." Leave him in peace! Leave him alone! All he wants is to stay home, and is not interested in invitations to parties, nor does he crave worldly success. This is sometimes due to nervousness (as in my case and that of any others), as well as the urge to concentrate without distraction on creative work. If this bothers you, my "protectors", you have a thousand ways of stopping me, but if it is useful, then none of your hirelings, however expert, can match my innate abilities and my sincerity. So leave minds and talents to do their work among us – not on a leash, but free to get on with their work whatever it may be. Don't force them to go in any direction other than that of their own choosing. If they are honest and sincere, they will make the right choice – which will be of benefit to Russia. Only then will Russia grow to take its rightful place alongside other nations! There is no doubt that people of the right stature will emerge – in science and in art – and provide the momentum to propel our country in a different, unexpected and, of course, right direction! I am confident of this – and I am surprised that, in the midst of these temporary setbacks, anyone can doubt the bright and clear future awaiting mankind. That would mean losing faith in Providence.

As far as I myself, my insignificant affairs and indeed my destiny are concerned, throughout the sorry story of the betrayal of my trust by Turgenev, who revealed my intentions to foreigners, and the campaign against me waged by that "gang of tormentors", I am learning the lessons of Providence, and I bless its justice, wisdom and goodwill. I was heedless of two warnings from the Gospels, and was lazy and careless in the use of my talents.

I squandered them, and they were stolen from me and handed over to "someone who possessed two talents"!

Later, in my anger, I failed to forgive him my first debt and referred to it somewhat indignantly, and in this way I paid off all my debts.

I am copying here some parts of the few letters I still have from Turgenev, where he happens to refer to my novels in passing. After my reconciliation with him I burned most of them. Only four or five were left. I don't know if they are still in my desk somewhere, but, in case they are lost, here are a few sentences. (I don't know whether the whole of this manuscript will reach the next generation, and if it will fall into well-meaning and impartial hands. If it doesn't, it won't matter and so be it.)

"How are your literary activities getting on?" Turgenev wrote from Paris on 11th November 1856. "I would hate to think that you have set aside your golden pen. I tell you what Mirabeau once told Sieyès: '*Le silence de M. Gontcharoff est une calamité publique*'.* I am sure that, in spite of how busy you must be with your job as a censor, you are still finding time for your real work, and the few words you spoke to me before I left give me grounds to hope that all is not lost. And I shall still continue nagging you and shouting the word 'Oblomov' in your ear, not to mention your second novel – the one about the artist – until you finish work on both of them, if only to get me off your back! I mean it – you will see! All joking aside, I beg you to let me know where you are with those two novels. My great enthusiasm for your project I feel gives me the right to offer a little suggestion!"

A few lines further on Turgenev adds: "I intend to get to know the writers here and try to take a more active part in French life."

A few months before this letter he wrote to me (from the village of Spasskoye* on 21st June 1856) in the same vein. "Incidentally," he writes, "I have been thinking to myself (and consoling myself at the same time) that, though you have to be in St Petersburg and work as a censor, I'm sure you can take the time to continue your novel on the side – that is to say, finally complete *Oblomov* and make a start on your next novel, from which I expect 'heaps of gold', although perhaps I shouldn't have put it that way. What I meant was that I don't want it to be thought that I bought it from you – well, anyway, I'm sure you understand me. I still remember a dinner in St Petersburg in my flat at which you talked to me and Dudyshkin about some details in your novel. It would be a sin to let all that material go to waste!"

In his next letter from Paris of 11th–23rd November, where he says how upset he was by my letter complaining about depression and how I was unable to write, etc., he continues: "I think that when you complain about yourself you deliberately exaggerate in order to irritate and goad yourself (a feeling with which I couldn't be more familiar), but your letter expresses such unfeigned earnestness and sincerity that I can only shrug my shoulders. Must we really, I felt, give up on Goncharov the author? Are we really ready to see this delightful novel – which was outlined in a single winter evening in St Petersburg (at Stepanov's place) and which filled Dudyshkin and myself with such a warm, cheerful feeling (you haven't forgotten that evening?), a novel which, almost completed, was about to make its appearance – are we ready, I repeat, to see it disappear into thin air?" He went on to say that he would have liked to be a pretty young woman, who could persuade me to make it a rule to write for an hour a day and so on.

In a letter from Paris of 8th–20th March, apparently written in response to the announcement of my intention to finish *Oblomov*, he himself complains of depression and a painful bladder, and adds "in reproaching you for idleness, I was an ass to pester you and ask you 'Why aren't you writing?' And I was quite affected by this myself – I was even rather repelled by the thought that I myself had once poured my own homegrown oil into that unwieldy machine known as Russian literature!"

So much bonhomie and genuine concern for both my novels, *Oblomov* and *Raisky* (*The Same Old Story* had already been published in 1847)! But this was just diplomatic language which betrayed an impatience to find out whether I'd write and finish something myself in time, or, to quote the first letter itself, "What's the status of both of my novels", in order to find out how far I had got and whether or not he had time to include the chapters "borrowed" from *Raisky* in *A Nest of the Gentry*, and to hand over the episode of Kozlov and his wife to one of his French literary figures with whom he was friendly at the time.

All of this became common knowledge subsequently: *A Nest of the Gentry* and *Madame Bovary* had unquestionably already been written in 1856 or 1857 and published the following year!* Such coincidences are no accident: it must be a matter of one person imitating another. Turgenev was at his most artful and had anticipated the sequence of events; he knew that I couldn't take him to court, and this only emboldened him. I didn't know of the existence of *Madame Bovary* until 1868 or 1869, when *Malinovka* was published – in fact, hardly anyone of us had heard of this French novel, and it was only after the publication of *Malinovka* that an unseen hand had at that time made the Russian public aware of *Madame Bovary*. And it was only in 1870 that *Sentimental Education* equally mysteriously found its way into the same journal in January or February. "Well, what do you think of that – it's almost the same! It must have been 'borrowed' by the Frenchman! Who else but the great Flaubert!" And he started people whispering everywhere how, out of envy, after he had done his "borrowing" and we had fallen out, I persisted in continuing my novel! Following this "borrowing" and our falling-out, he proclaimed a school of "extreme realism", with Flaubert and, of course, himself as its founders. This idea he propagated through the Frenchman Courrière, author of *The History of Russian Literature*, which had been dictated to him by Turgenev, who was declared the unequivocal creator of a new school. The book includes the following words: "Turgenev writes from his head, and Goncharov from his heart" – praise, naturally, for his idol. "Writes from his head" means composing, and "writes from his heart" means creating, which is the essence without which there can be no art. In art, "heart" means imagination, humour, feeling! Without it, the school of extreme realism is therefore a mere fabrication designed to justify the absence of talent, the lack of creativity, so well illustrated in novels such as *Sentimental Education* and the latest works of Turgenev, which purport to be nothing but the naked truth, totally devoid of poetry or colour. They are lifeless, dry and dull, and alienate readers. We have Émile Zola complaining in a critical article that Flaubert's *Sentimental Education* had gone unnoticed. And why not! It is second-hand and distorted, so how could it have a live, warm and immediate effect on anyone? And the same goes for Turgenev's copies, lifeless and bloodless as they are in *Smoke*, *On the Eve* and elsewhere! No matter how hard you try to represent it as a "new school"! There are details and sparks of talent here and there, but taken together they amount to nothing.

There are madmen who try to unload their madness onto others!

Turgenev is eaten up with envy; it is only envy of such vehemence that could have dreamt up and carried out such a plot, which consumed twenty years of his life and dominated his writing. Can you imagine rearranging, cutting and rephrasing conversations and whole scenes, and coming up with felicitous sentences, similes, and trying to make his pygmies into a likeness of fully-fledged persons – both for himself and for others? And to live abroad for this purpose! Only a gigantic ego can endow a man with such enormous patience.

With what cunning deliberation he refers in his letter to *one particular gathering* at his home when I recounted my novel in the presence of Dudyshkin. Yet of our meeting alone together in my house... not a word about this in his letter! So that if, later on, I had tried to expose him, he would, of course, have claimed that he had heard what I had said in Dudyshkin's presence, although perhaps not everything, and that was what he had been referring to. But the deaths of Dudyshkin and Druzhinin had given him a free hand, and Stasyulyevich, of course, had told him that I had also burnt the letters!

And, of course, he began to act increasingly in the open, and, so it seemed to me, turned the whole story inside out and went around telling people, especially abroad, that "I" (in other words "he") had written all this (just like Khlestakov, who publishes every journal and even wrote *Yuri Miloslavsky*!)* – and, if you please, that it was someone else who was the envious one and who was drawing on "my" miniatures and making full-length novels out of them.

Even among us here there were those who trusted him, helping him to get hold of my notebooks and even conspiring to win over that Jew, Auerbach, but Turgenev had on the sly already succeeded in putting a Russian collar around the Frenchman's neck! He was biding his time and worrying about whether I would be writing something. From one point of view this would, of course, mean his exposure, but on the other hand it would allow him once again to draw material both for himself and others, and probably to say that all of this had been told to me by him! And that was the reason why he had been keeping such a close watch on me, trying to arrange a meeting with me and attempting to keep track of my movements through Stasyulyevich and his other stooges and henchmen. I now conclude this pitiful and distasteful story by shaking my pen clean. I'm not even going to take the trouble of rereading or correcting what I have written. Just leave it the way it is! However clumsily written, it is the truth, even if, although I would hate to think of it, it should come to be read by others, with all its mistakes, repetitions and excessive length. I cannot entrust it to others, even for the purpose of making copies, for fear that in my lifetime other eyes may fall on this story. It is not my fault! The guilty party is the one who started it. I hesitated for a long time before committing this rubbish to paper. Will it be worth anyone's while to dig up this dirt and reveal the petty and miserable sides of a man's soul, someone with remarkable intellectual gifts, talent, education and a subtly attractive personality under the surface?

Of course, I wouldn't have lifted a hand in response to this distressing episode if, because of my silence, everything I have described here had not had such unfortunate repercussions for me personally! The web they have spun was so fine that I have borne in silence the burden of the mischief they have done me simply because my own naked truth could not overcome the meretricious lie – and if the truth were to emerge, it would not do so until sometime in the future and not in our lifetime, when we will be judged by others, not by his supporters or my enemies, but by impartial investigators and scholars! But even now and henceforth, I forgive him, and all those who so persistently, blindly and senselessly did me harm – either just for the fun of it or for suspecting me for something of which I am innocent, or even possibly for whatever it was I did to deserve it. It is my wish and hope that, as I have said, matters will not deteriorate to the point that it will become necessary for me to go ahead with what I have written here! May God forgive us all!

NOTE. I hereby instruct my heirs and all those into whose hands this manuscript may fall to use and publish whatever they deem necessary and possible – firstly, no earlier than five years after my death; secondly, only if it should happen that Turgenev or others should publish or assert (on the basis of similarity between my novels and those of Turgenev or any foreign novelists) that it was not they who "borrowed" from me, but that it was I who "borrowed" from them – or that I was "following in the footsteps of others"!

Otherwise, even if some similarity is discovered but no prejudicial opinion regarding any "borrowing" is expressed, then I request that this entire manuscript be burnt or consigned for safekeeping to the Imperial Public Library as material for the use of a future historian of Russian literature. I request this with the utmost earnestness and in the hope that this posthumous wish will be honoured!

It goes without saying that this manuscript must never fall into the hands of any of Turgenev's personal friends (or, rather, obedient servants), such as Stasyulyevich, Tyutchev or any member of that circle, who will do everything in their power to justify him

– and find me at fault. Currently there are no discerning and objective critics among us – although there are a good many intelligent ones, who, however, are publicists rather than critics. But it is only profound, discerning and impartial criticism which is capable of weighing, discussing and resolving an issue of this nature. And it is this alone which will tell us who is right and who is wrong, although not right now, but only in the future. And Turgenev's friends (or rather his lackeys – he has never had friends) will go on cheering for him and condemning me.

Ivan Goncharov. December 1875 and January 1876.

An Uncommon Story – Continued

July 1878. I had sealed the previous fifty sheets, thinking I would stop where I did. But in the course of the last two and a half years a great many things have happened which have bearing on this story, and now that I have started, I feel obliged to continue – for one reason alone: to ensure that what I have written here can serve the truth. This is important even in the smallest matter. If in literature the slightest biographical detail of a writer is valuable, providing information about his upbringing, his schooling, his character, activities and private life – since this can serve as material for the history of his time, or as an example and ultimately as a lesson to be learnt – then what I have written here can teach us something about our literary traditions.

For a long time I forgot about Turgenev and his mischief, longing only for peace and quiet in my old age, and shrugged off the way he was exalted in the press as our foremost writer and "our greatest realist", when he was compared by some with Shakespeare – his Asya with Ophelia, for example (Evgeny Markov* in his critical articles). But he didn't forget about me: even when he was living in Paris he continued to keep tabs on me through his henchmen to find out whether I was writing anything, calculating that, if I were, he would be sure to be kept informed about what I was writing, and would issue a warning by hastily writing a short story on the same subject to make it appear that I had been cashing in on his work, and that everything up to this point had been consistent with his falsifications. And whenever any of my work had come out ahead of his, he would produce an imitation of it or prompt his French accomplice to produce a "parallel" – and this would all look very convincing. Finally, he would keep himself informed about whether I was writing anything, so that if it turned out that I was, he would wait and see what transpired before resorting to his dirty tricks. But if I simply kept silent, then he would continue with his plan by boldly declaring himself the foremost writer and dubbing me the imitator who "borrowed" from him. He was frantic, rushing around like a man obsessed, unable to sit still. *He's taken off, like a fugitive on the run from his numerous pursuers!* Of course, like anyone with a bad conscience, he feels that he is alone and that everyone knows he is a villain. He stops at nothing in his efforts to promote himself and to prove beyond the shadow of a doubt that it is *I* who am following in *his* footsteps and "borrowing" from him. He continues to have me watched by his henchmen in the hope that I will blurt something out to someone about this whole story, so that he can once again demand a formal meeting and legal evidence, and since there is none, he will triumphantly prove that I am a slanderer consumed by envy, and that he is a great writer and a victim.

But knowing all his tricks and dodges, I will keep my mouth shut, never ask anyone anything about him, never mention his works and never pester him. Of course, what he fears most of all is that my works may be translated into French. Spending so much time there in France as he does and cultivating his reputation as a genius and the leader of a school, he exerts tremendous influence on the new French writers, and does his level best to prevent the publication of the works of myself and others in French – mostly mine! This is first and foremost in order to hide the similarity of certain French novels for which he has provided material – which, he would have us believe, he has supplied out of sheer generosity – and secondly because of the possibility that a clever and insightful critic might crop up who could figure out what was original material and what was counterfeit, and also what was the product of its native soil and what was imported. He even went so far as to advise others who they should translate and how, and offer his own rating of our writers, a rating from which they suffered! For example, he and Flaubert translated a few selections from Tolstoy, but so far at least they have been careful not to touch his major works. "There's only one writer in Russia, and that's Turgenev – the rest are run-of-the-mill!" Only recently in a speech at a literary conference (of which more anon), he declared that Russia had four writers: Karamzin,* Pushkin, Lermontov and Gogol... "Don't forget Turgenev!" people shouted from the audience. Turgenev bowed in acknowledgement.

Incidentally, he lives in Paris and is afraid to leave it for fear that *War and Peace*, *Anna Karenina*, *The Cossacks* – and the works of Ostrovsky, Pisemsky, Saltykov-Shchedrin and many others – might be translated. If so, people would see how this genius paled into insignificance in comparison with all these luminaries. And if I too had been translated, people would have seen the source from which he appropriated so much material for himself and others!

They would probably have discovered whether or not the last two parts of *Malinovka* actually *were* worse than the previous ones, as he had assured his whole circle of acolytes, who were spreading this criticism more widely (because I had already stopped seeing him while I was writing them, thus making it impossible for him to lie about his helping me with his advice).

The voice of authority often has the effect of blinding the mass of people; they take him at his word and repeat his verdict, to which they eventually become accustomed until a genuine judge emerges and shows things in their true light. If Turgenev could cast the end of my novel in a false light by his wilfully damaging criticism and at the same time by lavishing exaggerated praise on the novels of Flaubert (which he was not doing in order to inflate Flaubert's reputation. At the time, they were working together to concoct a couple of stories, something to do with Herodias, and another about some saint or other – I don't remember which one. They had also written a short story, 'Un cœur simple'.* All of it was very bad and weak, and cannot serve as evidence that *Madame Bovary*, *Sentimental Education* and these stories were written by the same pen. The last two stories were nevertheless quite different from all the other works of this talentless Frenchman, pieced together on Turgenev's orders from the novels of other authors!). This could have happened only in Russia, where he has a gang of trained hounds and henchmen, but it couldn't be guaranteed to work abroad in spite of all the ties between him and the latest French writers. Finally, in both England and Germany there were people who could read French, possibly capable of discerning the truth.

And so, he would sooner put his hand in a fire than see translations from Russian into French, and is keeping a close watch from where he is sitting in order to prevent that happening.

This, by the way, is precisely what he has done. Last spring, in 1877, I received a letter from abroad from someone called Charles Deulin,* which began *"Monsieur et cher Maître"*, etc. He writes that eighteen years ago, soon after the publication of *Oblomov*, I granted him and his friend, M. De Lafitte (the pseudonym of a Russian, Pyotr Artamov, who was living in Paris) the right (*une autorisation*) to translate *Oblomov*, of which they had translated only the first part. Then De Lafitte/Artamov abandoned the translation, attended to another task and later died, and here was Charles Deulin, who didn't know a word of Russian, taking over and publishing (after eighteen years, mind you!) only that first part and sending me an author copy, accompanied by the most fulsome compliments, adding that even the French press was praising the book.

Soon afterwards I received the book itself. The translation turned out to be accurate and faithful – hardly surprising: Deulin wrote in the foreword that a whole colony of Russians had translated every expression. But the trouble was that the first part was only an introduction to the novel – it contained the comic repartee between Oblomov and Zakhar, but not the body of the novel itself: it lacked Olga and Stoltz and the subsequent development of Oblomov's character. The remaining three parts were left untranslated, while that first part was published as a separate work. What an outrage! I immediately recognized the hand of Turgenev in this, particularly when I saw on the title page in tiny print: *"Tous droits réservés"*,* which meant that no other translator had the right to translate or publish *Oblomov*, at least the first part.

They had figured it all out: without the first part, who would bother to translate the other three?

In his letter, Deulin added that he didn't know what to do with the first part, not knowing who to turn to. He said it was no use contacting Turgenev, since he was about to return to Russia – and there was nothing he could tell him. Turgenev had indeed returned to St Petersburg: I hadn't seen him, because I had long since broken off with him.

As to why Deulin hadn't turned to myself – that is something that perhaps Turgenev would know.

I replied to this Charles Deulin (he was turning out little stories from time to time such as *Buveurs de la bière*)* that if, eighteen years ago, I had in fact (something which I had forgotten) granted him the right to translate *Oblomov*, then it must have been not for an excerpt, but for the whole novel. He had only translated its introductory part, but not the novel itself, thus spoiling it for its French readers. In fact, this right had been granted to his friend who knew Russian, and not to him alone, and I certainly hadn't given him the right to include the inscription in Part One of "*Tous droits réservés*", thus preventing others from translating the rest of the novel. All this could only have been done, I added, by a malignant and jealous rival who had fed him this idea, although he must have carried it out without meaning to do me harm. (This correspondence is among my papers.)

In response, I received an aggrieved letter (from which I guessed what was afoot) asking me why I was making so much fuss about how strictly the conditions of the translation were being met, informing me that, in France, foreign authors were used to being treated in a cavalier fashion, and that I should consider myself lucky even to have become known to the French public and so on. And regarding the use of the expression "*Tous droits réservés*"... not a word! However, in this letter he admitted that Turgenev had offered him advice or suggested some correction (in an outrageous, absurd and misleading "Preface"), while in the first letter he had written that Turgenev had done nothing! In response, I wrote briefly to him and the book's publisher, Didier (who had also written to me), that I found it inappropriate to publish only the first part of a novel, and pointed out in particular that they had no right to include the inscription "*Tous droits réservés*" – and finally that I had granted translation rights to others.

Turgenev wanted to prevent the translation of the whole of *Oblomov* because French readers would inevitably realize that both that novel and *Malinovka* were the product of the same mind, imagination and pen, that between the two works there was a close kinship and similarity, that Raisky was a kind of Oblomov, that the whole setting is purely Russian and that the novels are set in a similar period.

It would therefore become apparent that I had not "borrowed" *Malinovka* from Flaubert, and that this novel had been patched together from scraps using a living thread and transplanted by someone onto French soil – and that the naturalist school had been grafted on from a previous Russian school... by a zealous Russian gardener!

And much would now be revealed that would cause that genius, Turgenev, great discomfiture, which was why he had been at such pains to hide Russian literature from the French!

And perhaps even from *Oblomov* he had managed to mine a good deal for inclusion in some French novel or other: a translation would, I suppose, reveal this and create a scandal, an éclat, which might force the truth into the open!

However, in the spring of last year, 1877, I received a visit from two Frenchmen – a M. Lacoste and, I believe, a M. Grevin (he and his wife are both writers), who asked me if they could translate *Oblomov* or write some articles about it in the French papers. I replied that I was unwilling to intrude on foreign literature, but that they could do as they wished.

Turgenev was in St Petersburg at the time. One day P.V. Annenkov, who also happened to be here, called on me. I told him of the intention of the two Frenchmen to translate *Oblomov*. He, of course, reported this to Turgenev. It so happened that Turgenev had decided to return home to Russia, but rushed back to Paris obviously in order to put a stop to all this. Undoubtedly he succeeded, because this Frenchman's plan was at that point very vague. Turgenev in any case had intended to return to revel in his triumph, following the publication of his last novel, *Virgin Soil*. In the last few years he has continued to write trifles such as 'A Strange Story', 'Knock, Knock, Knock', 'The Brigadier', etc., and has even come out with a feeble version of *King Lear*. All of it is vapid and worthless, but he feels that it is necessary to show that he is constantly writing. I, however, had supposedly long since stopped writing, and therefore he couldn't possibly be suspected of plagiarism, and it followed, therefore, that I must have been the one "borrowing" from him and not vice versa. It was to this end that he decided to write a major novel and produced *Virgin Soil*.

Towards the end of my *Malinovka* there is a reference to a "Party of Action", but the particular party is not specified, except for a vague suggestion that it might be a young party of propagandists who are wrought up about something and are preparing to take some action. In the character of Tushin there is a representative of a healthy, sturdy and businesslike generation who takes an active interest in the forest that he owns – and later falls in love with Vera, in spite of her "downfall" and all that business, and is preparing to marry her. Turgenev proved very skilful in dealing with this and changed my Tushin into Solomin, who also marries a woman who has left someone else, but portrayed the party of action in full swing – in the person of Nezhdanov and others – and even made use of the last words of *Malinovka* for his own purpose. All of this was skilfully camouflaged and deliberately muddled, except that I could not be fooled, since I was the author and knew the whole thing by heart.

But the impact of *Virgin Soil* was not at all what he had expected. It was feeble, pitiful and abject! It was just a heap of worms milling around something, like something cut out of a piece of paper, or silhouettes of manikins, bereft of any features or morality. It was all colourless, dreary, lifeless and drab, like cheap wallpaper. The figures were conventional, as were the action and the dialogue. In a word, extremely "realistic", as Flaubert and his crew would describe them.

This was how it was all viewed by the public, which was taken aback, and expressed its disappointment – a disappointment unanimously shared by the press, who did not mince their words! Probably many of those to whom he lied about me, saying I was jealous of him and stole his ideas, may have entertained doubts and wondered whether it was true. But didn't the opposite turn out to be true? Why did his stories, *A Nest of the Gentry* and *Fathers and Children* – especially the former – turn out to be so entertaining and well written (at the time when he was eavesdropping on me and extracts from my notebook were being delivered to him on the sly), while all his other works, after those extracts were no longer available to him, were simply worthless? He had already published the "parallel" to the first part of *The Same Old Story* in his *Torrents of Spring*, where he changed the setting to Frankfurt, adding the character of a young "coquette", which is successful and shows real talent – the rest was modelled on my idea, scattered here and there in the text. In my book, a young man is in the throes of first love and drenched in the vernal tears of youth, in his a young woman – in mine it's the heroine who betrays, in his the hero! Also "borrowed" from me is the horse-riding scene – purely incidental in my version, whereas he goes to town on it! Nor does Turgenev neglect details: his heroine washes berries like my Nadenka – and that business of the duel is along the very same lines!

In the last issue of *Vestnik Evropy* (August 1878), he slipped in an extract from the 'Notes' or 'Memoirs of a Writer' by Élie Berthet,* where a similar method of "borrowing" from his friends is attributed to the French writer Ponson du Terrail.* This excerpt has become one more weapon in Turgenev's arsenal to be used against me, having satisfied himself that I have given up writing. He has made this insinuation so that he can then claim (after circulating to the French extracts from my works before they have been published, since he had advance knowledge of them from having overheard them as well as from actually having read my notebooks) that I had been doing exactly the same thing to French writers as I had to him. Quite possibly he is not actually doing this himself, but rather giving others the idea.

This is a strategy of which he is undoubtedly a past master. At the literary conference in which he had played such an active part, he unquestionably, because of his high standing in their ranks (he had revealed to them the new path of the naturalist school), he supported, perhaps even created, a new level of literary achievement, known as "*adaptation*" – and he has now come here, so I have heard, urging the government to have this item included in a final resolution. And now other writers who have succumbed to his influence will be telling people that the extracts from my works which he has distributed to them have actually been "borrowed" from *them*! And it is precisely by doing this kind of thing that he really is a genius! And he will probably succeed – and there's nothing I can do about it! Just throw up my hands and shut up! He has a whole crowd of so-called friends. I don't: I have lived – and will no doubt die – in isolation.

Meanwhile, Turgenev has been anticipating that, with this particular novel, *Virgin Soil*, he will finally prove that even without *Malinovka* he has written a major novel, whereas I am no longer writing and that consequently... etc., etc.

Unfortunately for him, the publication of this novel has coincided with an investigation of political chicanery, undertaken by the Senate. They have picked up about a hundred people, suspected of propagating social ideas and circulating forbidden books in the villages and the countryside. The printed protocol of this court case was to all intents and purposes a copy of *Virgin Soil* – or, rather, *Virgin Soil* was a copy of it.

Then Turgenev announced that he did not intend to continue writing – no doubt to the disappointment of his fans! At present he is attending a literary conference which is taking place at the same time as the current Paris Exhibition.* Edmond About* was sending out invitations (and I received one). Victor Hugo was presiding over the conference, and Turgenev was elected the chairman of the foreign delegates. I haven't yet seen a copy of the programme for the conference, but in the pamphlet 'The Voice' (July 12th this year) I read a letter from Paris written by a correspondent concerning the outrageous insolence with which the conference committee, in its ruling on the issue of copyright, imposed a ban not only on authors' translations into a foreign language, but also on all counterfeits and "*adaptations*", that is to say, appropriations of ideas and plot lines!

That's sheer craziness! In every literature authors constantly come up with similar ideas. How can anyone distinguish them and impose limitations on them like that? So if Molière wrote *Tartuffe*, *L'Avare*, etc., then no one is to dare touch the same plot! This would give rise to interminable squabbling!

There can be no doubt that Turgenev's hand has been slily at work here, trying to prevent the translation into French of those Russian works (including my own) which he has long since already handed over to French writers! Well, good for him! Of course, who could ever think that, because of the creepy, underhand machinations of a jealous man who has insinuated himself opportunely into a foreign literature, some Frenchman, some Flaubert or other, could take whatever is good from Russian literature, from the works of that man's rival? And who do you think that was? Turgenev! Such a good-natured, honest fellow! Oh, what a cunning fox he was! But what God does not provide, the pig will not eat!

Perhaps, in this case, he also had some other purpose in mind – who can tell? In any case, his purpose was not good – he was sacrificing the interests of Russian literature on the altar of French literature! This is all very upsetting and sickeningly stupid! This is all I have to say for the time being.

I. Goncharov, July 1878

Note to *An Uncommon Story*

The manuscript of *An Uncommon Story* should be dealt with according to my instructions at the end of the last sheet.

August 1878

It would make me very happy to know that this manuscript (*An Uncommon Story*) will never need to be published – not only in the press, but even for the benefit of a small circle of writers or other persons. I feel like throwing it into the fire, even if everything set forth in it is the honest truth, at the thought of any outsider seeing it after my death. The need to tell a true story alone is not sufficient reason for writing these pages, if anyone is to suffer from their content: there is something higher than the truth – that is to forget and forgive an evil deed. How happy it would make me to satisfy my heart's desire, but that would mean accepting what was done by my enemy. If he didn't do everything I have described, that would make me the villain – that is what he set out to do, and it placed us both in an untenable position. But I cannot assume the burden of his guilt, his jealousy, his incorrigible lies, the misappropriation of someone else's property, all the accusations and slander heaped upon me.

Finally, if he had stopped, leaving things as they are now – let people think and say covertly that I am his imitator following in his footsteps, let him be praised to the skies both here and abroad as a genius (as indeed they are now doing) – I would have stayed silent, as I am doing now, however much they are tearing me apart, forcing me to come out into the open and giving him the opportunity to rebut me with the help of his crowd of cronies, agents and obedient hangers-on and so on. But he goes further, he wants to create some *éclat* or other, so as to entrench more deeply in the public mind and the press that *I*, not him, am the one who is consumed with jealousy, who takes someone else's property. He continues to build up his stockpile of weapons, even though right now, both here and abroad, people believe him to be not only the foremost, but virtually the only Russian literary figure alive.

That is not enough for him. He has long been smuggling into foreign novels all that I have written, copying my manuscripts in their entirety or in part – and, what is worse, when there was nothing left for him to plunder, he started on his own feeble and worthless stuff such as *Virgin Soil*, along with a number of other minor and vacuous stories. Probably, while craftily deceiving me and duping me with his dirty tricks, many of those whom he had taken in have begun to entertain doubts and to open their eyes to his lies, to come to their senses and distinguish between the truth and his lies and chicanery – and in the mean time rumours have begun to spread and people have begun talking. He is moving heaven and earth to prevent the truth from getting out. His crowd of blind supporters and lickspittles and toadies with whom he has surrounded himself like a protective wall – many, of course, in all innocence, some under the spell of his talent, others misled by his superficial bonhomie and good humour – have risen up against me in a mass. He is well aware of this, and is relentlessly pursuing his objective.

Having blocked access by foreigners to the whole of Russian literature and my works in particular, he has made it his business, living in Paris, to see to it that no one at all has translated any major works (such as those by Tolstoy, Ostrovsky and others), because translations of their works might make people aware of the solidity of Russian literature, while translations of my novels might bring to light strange similarities to certain novels, and God knows where that might lead... To put a stop to this once and for all, he has been more insistent than anyone that the literary conference should adopt the clause on "*adaptation*". That is to say that all similarities should be ruled out. Consequently, if this rule concerning similarities were to be included in the final resolution, then translations of my works would be out of the question, because he has already conveyed both the content and, to some extent, the structure of my novels. In this way, it would appear that it wasn't the French "borrowing" from a Russian author, but *him* "borrowing" from *them*.

To this end he arranged things in such a way that only the first part of *Oblomov* was translated into French, under a different title, while three parts were left untranslated. I therefore conclude that they have long ago been transplanted into some novel or other – which one I cannot say. After finishing work on *Oblomov* in Marienbad in 1857 (three parts, that is), I left for Paris, where I found Turgenev, Botkin (Vasily Petrovich) and Fet, who married Botkin's sister on the day of my arrival. At one sitting I read everything that had been written to Botkin and Turgenev. Now, that was when Turgenev had heard everything, and two years later I published it in the journal *Otechestvenniye Zapiski*.

And now, if the other parts come to be translated, he will misrepresent the author of the novel as nothing but a puppet, and will say that it was I who had been "borrowing" from him. And I imagine that if everything they have concocted at the literary conference is included in the final resolution, then someone will have to be rewarded for the idea or its implementation, depending on what Ivan Sergeyevich has been dishing out to this and that.

Before *Malinovka* was published, I knew only that Turgenev had been "borrowing" from me, and from that novel in particular, and I published it almost against my will, since I was under pressure from so many quarters. And the particular reason why I had not wanted to do this was precisely because I knew that it had already been ransacked by him. But what I did not suspect was that he had long since been sharing the stolen goods with others. In 1855 I had recounted the novel to him and, in 1859 or 1860, Flaubert's *Madame Bovary* had already been published (Kozlov and his wife, in my book). By then Turgenev had all but settled in Paris.

But I knew nothing of that until I read *The Country House on the Rhine*, which had been published at the same time as *Malinovka* in *Vestnik Evropy*. The same structure, the same setting and many similar characters. I was astounded. When I pointed out to Turgenev this similarity and the foreword he had concocted, he said that it had been drafted by others, and that all he had done was to sign it.

Then in 1870, after the publication of *Malinovka*, under the heading "Foreign Belles-Lettres", something called "Contemporary French Society", a translation of Flaubert's *Sentimental Education*, appeared in *Vestnik Evropy*. Here I was even more taken aback by the similarity – nothing more or less than a paraphrase of *Malinovka*. To begin with, I skimmed through it here and there, but suddenly near the end I came upon the last words of the translator – someone called Solovyov, although it could easily have been the work of Turgenev himself, who at that time was pretty well hand-in-glove with Stasyulyevich, together with whom he started to prepare for battle. It stated clearly that Flaubert's character, Fréderic, appears to bear some resemblance to Raisky, and that they are essentially one and the same person. I then got hold of the French original, read it, and finally, although late in the day, realized how badly I had been let down by what I had believed to be a true friend – and what that person really thought about me.

So it was then that, seeing how it was all going to end and what was in store for me and my work, I repented bitterly – not just for my gullibility, which was due to my insecurity and eternal (and still present) doubts in my own abilities (which is why I read my writings to everyone and shared my thoughts with them) – but also regretted the fact that I had been fated to become a writer, and not something else: in any other career I might have been stripped of my property and others might have stood in my way if I had trodden the path of ambition. As it is, damage is being done to my unblemished good name, for that predator, having taken advantage of my trusting nature, which he had already betrayed, has thrown in his lot with foreign writers, given away what belonged to me to others and, of course, by so doing, tarnished my reputation. I am not going to bend my head like a sheep under the knife, and have made up my mind to defend my literary standing and my name by chronicling each successive step in detail in my relations with Turgenev, and describing how he has abused my trust and friendship.

He is still continuing on this path and biding his time before going public – and since, on the strength of his talent alone (including the talent of others he has appropriated), he will not succeed in maintaining the position which he has seized by underhand and crooked means, he is now going all out!

Everyone is against me: I have been living alone and have no friends. There are a few humble, non-literary acquaintances and, I would imagine, quite a few people, both unknown and known to me, who appreciate my work, but none of those who appreciate literature are writers themselves, and therefore cannot help me with any publicity. Old friends and contemporaries have died, and today's press consists of people who are not merely indifferent, but actually hostile to the older generation of writers, partly out of envy, and partly because literary ideas and tastes have changed so much, surrendering as they have to the trends of utilitarianism and extreme naturalism. True critical opinion has vanished entirely; if there is any left, it has been mollified by the sweet-tempered and smug Turgenev!

So I will be silent, and will not even publish any new editions of my novels, despite the requests of publishers. I would probably do better to shut up and stop making waves, from which Turgenev always emerges unscathed – while I am always the loser, because almost everyone is against me.

I believe God is on my side, although perhaps because of my sins I am not worthy!

I have always shied away from being translated into foreign languages, thinking that my writings were below par, and now I am even more reluctant, since I want to avoid a brouhaha, which Turgenev would welcome, because it would finally put paid to me!

Can it really be that lies and dirty tricks will prevail? I hope not, and that sooner or later the truth will out. May God grant that – if not for my sake, then for the sake of the truth! And it is this truth which is set forth in the manuscript I have been compiling little by little, should the need ever arise to make it public. Otherwise, I request my heirs to withhold publication.

Supplement to *An Uncommon Story*

June 1879. For two years Turgenev has been moving heaven and earth, terrified that his hypocrisy will come to light. He returned here for a short time to rally his supporters and recruit more cronies. After publishing *Virgin Soil*, remarkable only because it was so stale and boring (in doing so, he hoped to convince people that allegedly it was he who had been recounting everything to me), he practically went out of his mind for fear that he would finally be exposed. He couldn't afford to stay here for long, because it might become apparent that we no longer see each other. I am not saying people would start asking what that means, and perhaps not take his word for it. Once he heard that I was publishing all my works, he rushed back here and then hurried to Moscow to inveigle his friends – his stooges – into giving him a triumphal welcome. In Moscow, at the Society of Lovers of Literature, he was cheered by the students.

There was a dinner at Borel's here,* to which a number of professors and academics and others were invited, or dragged. That stupid Yakov Karlovich Grot* compared him with Pushkin, and Grigorovich, who is temperamentally incapable of jealousy, declared, apropos absolutely of nothing, that Turgenev was incapable of envy. This was said in case anyone ever suspected that Turgenev had been feeding my work along to French writers. And this great authority, Grigorovich, cautioned everyone against the idea of jealousy.

And his great triumph amounted to this: how could anyone suspect him of envy and plagiarism? Just try it! Well, he has figured it all out!

He had won over Grigorovich to his side – probably because he had heaped praise on his School of Drawing. In return for this, after vilifying him along with everyone else, he immediately became his vociferous supporter. Taking advantage of the Paris Exhibition, some French writers, under the chairmanship of Victor Hugo, came up with the idea of an international conference, supposedly to protect so-called literary property, in other words to collect fees from foreign literatures for translations and so-called "*adaptations*", something which was once again dreamt up, as we were told by those returning from Paris, by Turgenev. He was primarily responsible for promoting this idea, and since it was he who had brought over a whole literary school to them, they considered him a genius. He exerts tremendous influence, and everyone went along with this idea, in spite of the objections of Hugo and others.

This fraudster of ours had one goal in mind: to prevent translations of my work into French. There might be critics there, I suppose, who might have wondered where this work came from, and guessed that the illustrious Flaubert had plucked it from somewhere! So here he is, going all out to whip up publicity to avoid coming across as a plagiarist and a traitor – for which there are good grounds – instead of a genius! His attempts in Paris were a fiasco: he did not gain the writers' trust. So the conference was moved to London, and was attended by such distinguished figures as the Prince of Wales and Lord Beaconsfield,* who are taking an active part in the matter. Turgenev himself was now in hiding, and sent Grigorovich in his place – a loudmouth and a windbag who is now playing first fiddle in Turgenev's orchestra – and what good will come of it!

Et voilà comme on écrit l'histoire!

Notes

p. 3, *Belinsky and his circle of writers and friends*: The St Petersburg literary circle gathering around the influential Russian critic of Westernizing tendency Vissarion Belinsky (1811–48), who supported the work of many young writers, including Nikolai Nekrasov (1821–78), Ivan Turgenev (1818–83) and Fyodor Dostoevsky (1821–81). Dostoevsky famously showed his first novel *Poor People* to Belinsky in 1845, who hailed it as Russia's first "social novel".

p. 3, *Botkin and Annenkov*: The Russian essayist Vasily Botkin (1812–69) and the Russian memoirist and critic Pavel Annenkov (1813–87), a close friend of Turgenev.

p. 3, *Panayev, Grigorovich*: The Russian writers Ivan Panayev (1812–62) and Dmitri Grigorovich (1822–1900).

p. 3, *Druzhinin with his novella Polinka Saks*: The Russian novelist Alexander Druzhinin (1824–64), best remembered today for his epistolary novella *Polinka Saks* (1847).

p. 3, *Tyutchev, Maslov, Yazykov*: Nikolai Nikolayevich Tyutchev (1815–78), Ivan Maslov (1815–91) and Mikhail Yazykov (1811–85).

p. 3, *Maykov's, the poet's father*: Nikolai Maykov (1794–1873), father of the Russian poet Apollon Maykov (1821–97).

p. 3, *The Same Old Story*: Goncharov's first novel, published in 1847. *An Uncommon Story* is in ironic counterpoint to the title of this earlier work, which has also been translated in English as *A Common Story*.

p. 3, *Otechestvenniye Zapiski*: *Otechestvenniye Zapiski* ("Notes of the Fatherland") was a St Petersburg monthly literary journal published from 1818 to 1884, edited by Andrei Krayevsky (1810–89).

p. 4, *the Sovremennik*: The *Sovremennik* ("The Contemporary") was a literary journal published in St Petersburg from 1836 to 1866.

p. 4, *he had already published something in Otechestvenniye Zapiski*: Turgenev's narrative poem *Andrei* had been published in *Notes of the Fatherland* in 1845. Belinsky had also written a glowing review of Turgenev's long poem *Parasha* for the same journal in 1843.

p. 4, *an Onegin or a Pechorin*: Eugene Onegin and Grigory Pechorin are the Byronic heroes of Alexander Pushkin's eponymous novel in verse and Mikhail Lermontov's (1814–41) novel *A Hero of Our Time* (1840), respectively.

p. 4, *Stolypin (nicknamed "Mongo")*: Alexei Stolypin, a Russian officer from a prominent noble family, and a relative and friend of Lermontov.

p. 5, *revolution and a change of government in France*: A reference to the French Revolution of 1848.

p. 5, *Granovsky, Kavelin and Galakhov*: Timofei Granovsky (1813–55), Konstantin Kavelin (1818–85) and Alexei Galakhov (1807–92). Together with the Russian novelist and thinker Alexander Herzen (1812–70), they were among the most prominent supporters of Russia's Westernization.

p. 6, *Oblomov*: Goncharov's second and most famous novel, first published in 1859.

p. 6, *'Oblomov's Dream'*: This would later form Chapter 9 in Part One of the finished novel.

p. 7, *Malinovka Heights*: Goncharov's third and final novel (also translated in English as *The Precipice*), first published in 1869. Its hero is the dilettante artist Boris Raisky.

p. 7, *Memoirs of a Hunter*: A cycle of stories first published in 1852. Also translated in English as *A Sportsman's Sketches* or *Sketches from a Hunter's Album*, it was Turgenev's first major work of fiction.

p. 8, *A Nest of the Gentry... Smoke*: Four of Turgenev's most famous works of fiction, published in 1859, 1862, 1860 and 1867, respectively.

p. 8, *Admiral Putyatin*: The Russian admiral Yevfimiy Putyatin (1803–83).

p. 8, *The Frigate Pallada*: A travelogue first published in 1858.

p. 8, *his "war stories"*: The allusion is to Leo Tolstoy's *Sevastopol Sketches* (1855).

p. 8, *The Death of Ivan the Terrible*: A historical drama by the Russian poet, novelist and playwright Alexei Tolstoy (1817–75).

p. 9, *Prince Odoevsky's*: The Russian philosopher and short-story writer Vladimir Odoevsky (1803–69).

p. 9, *Kozhevnikov's house*: The house of a Russian officer where Goncharov lived from February 1855 until the following year.

p. 10, *Elizabeth*: Empress Elizabeth of Russia (1709–62), who reigned from 1741 to 1762.

p. 10, *Catherine the Great*: Empress of Russia from 1762 to 1796.

p. 10, *the Encyclopedists*: The Enlightenment writers Denis Diderot (1713–84) and Jean le Rond d'Alembert (1717–83), who were the chief editors of the *Encyclopedia, or a Systematic Dictionary of the Sciences, Arts and Crafts* (usually referred to as the *Encyclopédie*), a general encyclopedia published in France from 1751 to 1772.

p. 10, *Decembrist*: A member of a group of Russian revolutionaries who led an unsuccessful revolt against Tsar Nicholas I in December 1825.

p. 11, *j'ai vidé mon sac*: Literally, "I have emptied my sack" (French), but metaphorically, "I got everything off my chest".

p. 11, *Dudyshkin*: The Russian author and critic Stepan Dudyshkin (1821–66). He was one of the editors and the leading literary critic of *Otechestvenniye Zapiski* from 1860 to 1866.

p. 11, *Marienbad*: The German name of the Czech spa town of Mariánské Lázně.

p. 11, *a printer's sheet*: Around 40,000 characters (including spaces) or 8,500 words.

p. 12, *Fet*: The Russian poet Afanasy Fet (1820–92).

p. 12, *The Country House on the Rhine*: An 1869 novel by the German poet and novelist Berthold Auerbach (1812–82).

p. 12, *Pisemsky*: The Russian novelist Alexei Pisemsky (1821–81).

p. 13, *kidney trouble... in the Paris climate*: The allusion is to syphilis, a disease that can cause damage to the kidneys.

p. 14, *Ivan Sergeych*: The name and patronymic of Turgenev. Goncharov's use of the shorter form of the patronymic (as opposed to the more formal "Sergeyevich") denotes a degree of familiarity between him and Turgenev.

p. 15, *"Ma Solitude", "Mon Repos", "Mon Hermitage"*: "My Loneliness", "My Resting Place", "My Hermitage" (French).

p. 17, *Gogol*: The Russian novelist, playwright and short-story writer Nikolai Gogol (1809–52).

p. 20, *Richelieu or Metternich*: The French cardinal and statesman Armand Jean du Plessis, Duke of Richelieu (1585–1642) and the Austrian statesman and diplomat Klemens von Metternich (1773–1859).

p. 22, *Nikitenko*: The Russian historian, professor and censor Alexander Nikitenko (1805–77).

p. 24, *plagiat*: "Plagiarism" (Latin).

p. 24, *et pour cause*: "And for good reason" (French).

p. 24, *The protagonist was some Bulgarian*: Dmitry Insarov.

p. 24, *my novel*: Malinovka Heights.

p. 25, *Ostrovsky*: The Russian playwright Alexander Ostrovsky (1823–86).

p. 26, *near the Viardot family*: The family of Louis (1800–83) and Pauline (née García, 1821–1910) Viardot, with whom Turgenev had a long romantic relationship, and possibly an affair.

p. 26, *brusquement*: "Abruptly" (French).

p. 26, *Feoktistov*: The Russian writer, journalist and satirist Evgeny Feoktistov (1828–98).

p. 26, *The Brigadier*: Probably a reference to the famous comedy by the Russian playwright Denis Fonvizin (1745–92), although Turgenev also wrote a story of that title, written in 1867.

p. 29, *Torrents of Spring*: An autobiographical novella by Turgenev, written in 1870–71, but first published in 1872.

p. 29, *Vestnik Evropy*: Vestnik Evropy ("European Herald") was a St Petersburg literary journal published from 1866 to 1918.

p. 29, *his protagonist*: Dmitry Sanin.

p. 30, *'Hamlet of the Shchigrovsky District'*: An 1848 short story by Turgenev.

p. 31, *chef de la nouvelle école, comme romancier*: "Head of the new school, as a novelist" (French).

p. 31, *avec l'autorisation de l'auteur*: "With permission by the author" (French).

p. 32, *"Je ne doute pas de leur parfaite honorabilité"*: "I have no doubt at all about their perfect honesty" (French).

p. 32, *Flaubert*: The French novelist Gustave Flaubert (1821–80).

p. 34, *Histoire de la littérature russe by Courrière*: Histoire de la Littérature Contemporaine en Russie, an 1875 work by Céleste Courrière (1843–c.1890).

p. 34, *Woe From Wit*: An influential verse comedy by Alexander Griboyedov (1795–1829).

p. 36, *Golyadkin and Prokharchin*: Golyadkin is the hero of *The Double* and Mr Prokharchin that of an eponymous short story by

Dostoevsky. Both were published in 1846, the same year as *Poor People*.

p. 36, *House of the Dead*: A semi-autobiographical narrative published between 1860 and 1862.

p. 36, *Crime and Punishment*: Published in 1866.

p. 36, *The Carpenters*: *The Carpenters' Cartel*, a novel published in 1855.

p. 38, *Chapter 9*: In Part Two. She also features prominently in Part Two, Chapter 12.

p. 40, *Karlsbad*: The German name of the Czech spa town of Karlovy Vary.

p. 41, *Stasyulyevich*: The Russian historian and journalist Mikhail Stasyulyevich (1826–1911). From 1866 to 1908 he was the editor of *Vestnik Evropy*

p. 41, *Death of Ioann*: *The Death of Ioann Grozny* (1866).

p. 41, *Fyodor Ioannovich*: *The Tsar Fyodor Ioannovich* (1868).

p. 45, *'The Brigadier'*: An 1867 story by Turgenev.

p. 45, *Count Apraksin*: Viktor Apraksin (1822–98).

p. 48, *Bobchinskys and Dobchinskys*: Two characters in Gogol's comedy *The Government Inspector* (1836). They are the source of the initial unfounded rumours about the arrival in town of a government inspector.

p. 49, *Kovalevsky*: The Russian writer Pavel Kovalevsky (1823–1907).

p. 50, *"blue night"… left*: *Oblomov*, Part Four, Chapter 8.

p. 50, *"I am his bride!"*: Ibid., Chapter 4.

p. 52, *Makarov*: The Russian writer Nikolai Makarov (1826–92).

p. 54, *the Summer Garden*: A park in St Petersburg.

p. 54, *Karatygin*: The Russian actor Vasily Karatygin (1802–53).

p. 56, *Russkiy Vestnik*: *Russkiy Vestnik* ("The Russian Herald") was a St Petersburg literary journal published from 1856 to 1906, edited at the time by Mikhail Katkov (1817–87).

p. 59, *Reshetnikov*: The Russian writer Fyodor Reshetnikov (1841–71).

p. 60, *"My lovers… stand afar off"*: Psalms 38:11.

p. 62, *C'est impayable!*: "It's priceless!" (French).

p. 67, *P. O.*: Possibly Prince Odoevsky (see first note to p. 9).

p. 67, *que la littérature, c'est moi*: "That I am the literature" (French).

p. 69, *mœurs de province*: "Provincial life" (French). "*Mœurs de province*" is the subtitle (and original title, later discarded) of *Madame Bovary*.

p. 70, *Émile Zola*: The French naturalist novelist Émile Zola (1840–1902).

p. 71, "*Je ne vous en veux pas*": "I don't bear a grudge against you" (*Madame Bovary*, Part Three, Chapter 11).

p. 72, *Sentimental Education (1870 edition)*: *L'Éducation Sentimentale: Histoire d'un jeune homme* (Paris: Michel Lévy Frères, 1870).

p. 74, *Salammbô with its oriental setting*: An 1862 historical novel by Flaubert set in Carthage at the time of the Mercenary War of 241–237 BC.

p. 74, *probably in 1856*: *Madame Bovary* was serialized in the French literary journal *Revue de Paris* ("Paris Review") from October to December 1856, and published in book form in April 1857.

p. 76, "*Ah, je suis tranche canaille*": "I am an absolute scoundrel". The phrase does not appear in *Sentimental Education*.

p. 77, *Le Nord*: A French-language Russian journal published in Brussels (and later in Paris) from 1855.

p. 78, *George Sand*: The French novelist George Sand (1804–76).

p. 78, *Laroche*: The Russian music and literary critic Herman Augustovich Laroche (1845–1904).

p. 79, *Francia*: A novel first published in 1872.

p. 80, "*Nul n'est prophète chez soi*": "No one is a prophet in his own country" (French).

p. 80, *Farçeur!*: "Poseur!" (French).

p. 80, *Surovin*: The Russian journalist Alexei Surovin (1834–1912).

p. 80, *Saltykov-Shchedrin*: The Russian satirist Mikhail Saltykov-Shchedrin (1826–89).

p. 82, *the brothers Goncourt*: The French naturalist writers Edmond de Goncourt (1822–96) and Jules de Goncourt (1830–70).

p. 82, *The Temptation of St Anthony*: A drama novel published in 1874.

p. 83, *Libre penseur*: Freethinker (French).

p. 84, *corps et âme*: "Body and soul" (French).

p. 87, *Nedelya*: Nedelya ("The Week") was a literary magazine published in St Petersburg from 1866 to 1903.

p. 89, "*Roman pittoresque, immense talent*": "Picturesque novel, immense talent" (French).

p. 90, '*La littérature russe – c'est moi!*': "I am Russian literature!" (French).

p. 91, *the quarrel between two literary Ivan Ivanychs and Ivan Nikiforovichs*: The reference is to a famous short story by Nikolai Gogol, 'The Story of How Ivan Ivanovich Fell Out with Ivan Nikiforovich', published in the cycle *Evenings on a Farm Near Dikanka* (1831–32).

p. 91, *Old-World Landowners*: Another story by Gogol in the same cycle.

p. 92, *Pas si bête!*: "Nothing so stupid!" (French).

p. 93, *Et toutes les apparences sont contre moi*: "And everything appears to be against me" (French).

p. 93, *'To My Critics'*: The reference is evidently to Goncharov's article 'Better Late than Never' (1879).

p. 94, *"Audiatur et altera pars"*: "May the other side also be heard" (Latin).

p. 95, *"Oblomovism"*: "Oblomovism" (in Russian *oblomovshchina*) is a term created by the literary critic Nikolai Dobrolyubov (1836–61) in an influential article, analysing the character and shortcomings of Goncharov's *Oblomov*, 'What is Oblomovism?' (1859).

p. 95, *Germinie Lacerteux by the Goncourt brothers*: A novel by Edmond and Jules de Goncourt, first published in 1865.

p. 99, *some trouble with Count Tolstoy and a falling-out*: Turgenev and Tolstoy fell out in the early summer of 1861 over the way Turgenev was bringing up his daughter, among other reasons. The quarrel all but ended in a duel, and lasted for some seventeen years.

p. 99, *Count Alexei Tolstoy, who died last November*: See fifth note to p. 8.

p. 100, *succès d'estime*: "A critical success" (French).

p. 102, *Daudet*: The French novelist Alphonse Daudet (1840–97).

p. 102, *When I saw... into the German ocean*: The quotation is taken from Turgenev's introduction to his 'Literary and Personal Reminiscences' (1869).

p. 103, *Ogarev*: The Russian poet, historian and political activist Nikolai Ogarev (1813–77).

p. 107, *"La Russie – c'est le Japon"*: "Russia is like Japan" (French).

p. 108, *Orlov, Dolgorukov and Dubbelt*: Alexei Fyodorovich Orlov (1787–1862), Vasily Andreyevich Dolgorukov (1804–68) and Leontiy Vasilyevich Dubbelt (1792–1862), all head or managers of the Third

Section of His Imperial Majesty's Own Chancellery, a secret-police department set up in Imperial Russia.

p. 109, *Proudhon*: The French anarchist, politician and philosopher Pierre-Joseph Proudhon (1809–65).

p. 109, *Macaulay, Mignet and even Guizot were taboo*: The English historian and Whig politician Thomas Babington Macaulay (1800–59), the French journalist and historian François Mignet (1796–1884) and the French politician, historian and statesman François Guizot (1787–1874).

p. 110, *the Great Reformer*: The reference is to Tsar Alexander II (emperor from 1855 to 1881).

p. 110, *Nikolai Pavlovich*: Nikolai Pavlovich Romanov (Tsar Nicholas I), who was emperor of Russia from 1825 to 1855.

p. 111, *Peter*: Peter the Great.

p. 111, *"zemstvo"*: An organ of rural self-government in the Russian Empire.

p. 111, *A.G. Troynitsky*: Alexander Grigoryevich Troynitsky (1807–71), a high-ranking officer of the Russian Empire.

p. 113, *V.P. Titov*: The Russian writer and statesman Vladimir Pavlovich Titov (better known under the pseudonym "Tit Kosmokratov", 1807–91).

p. 113, *the late tsarevich*: Nikolai Alexandrovich (1843–65), the son of Tsar Alexander II.

p. 113, *It was in 1856, I believe... Glazunov*: Goncharov's travelogue, *The Frigate Pallada*, parts of which had been published in various literary journals between 1855 and 1857, was first published in volume form, under the imprint of Alexander Ilyich Glazunov (1829–96), in 1858.

p. 113, *Grand Duke Konstantin Nikolayevich*: Grand Duke Konstantin Nikolayevich (1827–92), the emperor's viceroy of Poland from 1862 to 1863, was Tsar Alexander II's younger brother.

p. 119, *bon gré, mal gré*: "Like it or not" (French).

p. 121, *"que c'est une calamité publique que je n'écris pas"*: "It's a disaster that I'm not writing anything" (French).

p. 121, *the Russian Teniers or Ostade*: The Flemish genre painter David Teniers the Younger (1610–90) and the Dutch painter and engraver Adriaen van Ostade (1610–85).

p. 122, *au courant*: "Up to date" (French).

p. 122, *audiatur et altera pars*: See note to p. 94.

p. 122, *à peu près*: "More or less" (French).

p. 123, *forced to give up... my employment*: At his own request, as a result of health complications, Goncharov retired from government service on 29th December 1867, at the age of fifty-five.

p. 123, *Mystificateurs et mystifiés (Bibliophile Jacob) par Michel Raymond*: "*The Mystifiers and the Mystified* (Bibliophile Jacob), by Michel Raymond" (French). The book, first published in 1875, is in fact by Paul Lacroix (1806–84), who wrote under the pseudonym of "Bibliophile Jacob" or "P.L. Jacob, bibliophile".

p. 124, *It all started with Chernyshevsky*: The Russian critic and novelist Nikolai Chernyshevsky (1828–89), author of the seminal novel *What Is to Be Done?* (1863).

p. 128, *sine ira*: "Without anger" (Latin).

p. 128, *Moskovskie Vedomosti*: *Moskovskie Vedomosti* ("Russian Gazette") was a Moscow literary journal published from 1756 to 1917.

p. 128, *Bakunin*: The Russian revolutionary anarchist Mikhail Bakunin (1814–76).

p. 129, *Journal de Saint-Pétersbourg*: A French-language newspaper published in St Petersburg from 1825 to 1914.

p. 130, *Chambord*: Henri, Count of Chambord and Duke of Bordeaux (1820–83) was the legitimist pretender to the throne of France from 1844.

p. 133, *Leskov*: The Russian prose writer Nikolai Leskov (1831–95).

p. 133, *The Diary of an Archpriest*: The reference is to Leskov's novel *The Cathedral Folk* (1872).

p. 133, *The Sealed Angel*: A novel by Leskov published in 1873.

p. 133, *Prince Meshchersky*: The Russian journalist and writer Vladimir Meshchersky (1839–1914).

p. 134, *some Lunins and Baburins*: A pun on the already mentioned title of Turgenev's story 'Punin and Baburin'. Goncharov replaces the first name with that of the Russian revolutionary Mikhail ("Michael") Lunin (1787–1845).

p. 136, '*Le silence de M. Gontcharoff est une calamité publique*': "Mr Goncharov's silence is a public calamity" (French). The French writer and statesman Honoré Gabriel Riqueti, comte de Mirabeau (1749–91), once famously said: "Le silence de l'abbé Sieyès est une calamité publique." Emmanuel Joseph Sieyès (1748–1836), usually known as the "Abbè Sieyès", was a Roman Catholic clergyman.

p. 136, *Spasskoye*: Spasskoye-Lutovinovo, Turgenev's childhood estate, around 10 km from Mtsensk, which he inherited after his mother's death in 1850.

p. 138, *published the following year!*: In fact, *Madame Bovary* was published in 1856 and *A Nest of the Gentry* in 1859.

p. 140, *just like Khlestakov, who publishes every journal and even wrote Yuri Miloslavsky*: Khlestakov is a character in Nikolai Gogol's *The Government Inspector* (1836). The historical novel *Yuri Miloslavski* (1829) is the best-known work of the Russian author Mikhail Zagoskin (1789–1852).

p. 143, *Evgeny Markov*: The Russian critic Evgeny Markov (1835–1903).

p. 145, *Karamzin*: The Russian historian and writer Nikolai Karamzin (1766–1826), widely regarded as one of the founding fathers of Russian literature.

p. 145, *'Un cœur simple'*: 'A Simple Heart', originally published in French in 1877 under the title *Trois contes* ("Three Tales") alongside 'Herodias' and 'St Julian the Hospitaller'.

p. 146, *Someone called Charles Deulin*: The French writer, theatre critic and folklorist Charles Deulin (1827–77).

p. 146, *"Tous droits réservés"*: "All rights reserved" (French).

p. 147, *Buveurs de la Bière*: "The Beer Drinkers" (French). Deulin's collection of short stories, published in 1868, is in fact called *Contes d'un buveur de bière* ("Tales of a Beer Drinker").

p. 150, *Élie Berthet*: The French writer Élie Berthet (1815–91), author of over a hundred novels.

p. 150, *Ponson du Terrail*: The French novelist Pierre Alexis de Ponson du Terrail (1829–71).

p. 151, *the current Paris Exhibition*: The "Exposition Universelle" ("World's Fair"), held in Paris from 1st May to 10th November 1878.

p. 151, *Edmond About*: The French novelist, publicist and journalist Edmond About (1828–85).

p. 159, *Borel's*: A well-known restaurant in St Petersburg, now closed.

p. 159, *Yakov Karlovich Grot*: The Russian philologist and translator Yakov Karlovich Grot (1812–93).

p. 160, *The Prince of Wales and Lord Beaconsfield*: The reference is to the Prince of Wales, the future King Edward VII (1841–1910), and to the English statesman, politician and writer Benjamin Disraeli, 1st Earl of Beaconsfield (1804–81), who served twice as British prime minister.

p. 160, *Et voilà comme on écrit l'histoire*: "And that is how history is written!" (French).

ALMA CLASSICS

ALMA CLASSICS aims to publish mainstream and lesser-known European classics in an innovative and striking way, while employing the highest editorial and production standards. By way of a unique approach the range offers much more, both visually and textually, than readers have come to expect from contemporary classics publishing.

LATEST TITLES PUBLISHED BY ALMA CLASSICS

473. Sinclair Lewis, *Babbitt*
474. Edith Wharton, *The House of Mirth*
475. George Orwell, *Burmese Days*
476. Virginia Woolf, *The Voyage Out*
477. Charles Dickens, *Pictures from Italy*
478. Fyodor Dostoevsky, *Crime and Punishment*
479. Anton Chekhov, *Small Fry and Other Stories*
480. George Orwell, *Homage to Catalonia*
481. Carlo Collodi, *The Adventures of Pinocchio*
482. Virginia Woolf, *Between the Acts*
483. Alain Robbe-Grillet, *Last Year at Marienbad*
484. Charles Dickens, *The Pickwick Papers*
485. Wilkie Collins, *The Haunted Hotel*
486. Ivan Turgenev, *Parasha and Other Poems*
487. Arthur Conan Doyle, *His Last Bow*
488. Ivan Goncharov, *The Frigate Pallada*
489. Arthur Conan Doyle, *The Casebook of Sherlock Holmes*
490. Alexander Pushkin, *Lyrics Vol. 4*
491. Arthur Conan Doyle, *The Valley of Fear*
492. Gottfried Keller, *Green Henry*
493. Grimmelshausen, *Simplicius Simplicissimus*
494. Edgar Allan Poe, *The Raven and Other Poems*
495. Sinclair Lewis, *Main Street*
496. Prosper Mérimée, *Carmen*
497. D.H. Lawrence, *Women in Love*
498. Albert Maltz, *A Tale of One January*
499. George Orwell, *Coming Up for Air*
500. Anton Chekhov, *The Looking Glass and Other Stories*
501. Ivan Goncharov, *An Uncommon Story*
502. Paul Éluard, *Selected Poems*
503. Ivan Turgenev, *Memoirs of a Hunter*
504. Albert Maltz, *A Long Day in a Short Life*
505. Edith Wharton, *Ethan Frome*
506. Charles Dickens, *The Old Curiosity Shop*
507. Fyodor Dostoevsky, *The Village of Stepanchikovo*
508. George Orwell, *The Clergyman's Daughter*
509. Virginia Woolf, *The New Dress and Other Stories*
510. Ivan Goncharov, *A Serendipitous Error and Two Incidents at Sea*
511. Beatrix Potter, *Peter Rabbit*

www.almaclassics.com